The Jews and the Crusaders

*The Hebrew Chronicles of the First
and Second Crusades*

BOHEMIA

Area of
map inset

Cologne

Wesseli

Aschaffenburg

Prague

Rouen

Mainz

Carentan

Metz

NORMANDY

Regensburg

Sully

Troyes

FRANCE

GERMANY

Clermont

ITALY

SPAIN

ATLANTIC OCEAN

MEDITERRA

First Crusade ••••••••••••••••••

⊗ Place attacked in First Crusade

⊘ Place of questionable attack -- First Crusade

Second Crusade ▬ ▬ ▬ ▬ ▬ ▬

⊠ Place attacked in Second Crusade

⊡ Place of questionable attack -- Second Crusade

0 100 200 300 400 500
Kilometers

0 100 200 300 400 500
Miles

The Jews
and the Crusaders

*The Hebrew Chronicles of the First
and Second Crusades*

Translated and edited by SHLOMO EIDELBERG

KTAV Publishing House, Inc.
Hoboken, New Jersey
1996

Paperback edition published by KTAV Publishing House, Inc.,
Hoboken, New Jersey, with permission, 1996

Library of Congress Cataloging-in-Publication Data

The Jews and the Crusaders : the Hebrew chronciles of the first and
second Crusades / translated and edited by Shlomo Eidelberg.
    p.   cm.
Previously published: Madison, Wis. : University of Wisconsin Press,
1977.
    Includes bibliographic references and index.
    Contents: The chronicle of Solomon bar Simson. The chronicle of
Rabbi Eliezer bar Nathan. The narrative of the Old Persecutions, or Mainz
anonymous. Sefer Zekhirah, or The book of remembrance, of Rabbi
Ephraim of Bonn.
    ISBN 0–88125–541–6
    1. Jews—Germany—History—1096–1147—Sources. 2. Jews—
Persecutions— Germany—Sources. 3. Crusades—First, 1096–1099—
Sources. 4. Crusades—Second, 1147–1149—Sources. 5. Germany—
History—843–1273— Sources. I. Eidelberg, Shlomo, 1918– .
DS135.G31J48   1996
943'.09424—dc20   96–253
                                       CIP

Manufactured in the United States of America
KTAV Publishing House, 900 Jefferson Street, Hoboken NJ, 07030

In memory of our greatly beloved son Daniel Coloman
October 19, 1962–July 8, 1971
21 Tishri 5723–15 Tammuz 5731

Contents

Illustrations

Preface

This work represents the outgrowth of my early studies at the
Hebrew University in Jerusalem. Perhaps of greatest stimulus were
the seminars of Professors I. F. Baer, B. Z. Dinur and R. Köbner, in
which a love for the history of the Jews in Western Europe was first
nurtured.

For many years I have wished to bring the moving epic of the
Hebrew chronicles of the Crusades to the English reader, not only to
the student and to the scholar, but to the educated layman, often
neglected in modern academic works. It is my hope that the presentation of these chronicles in this volume will serve not only as
groundwork for further research in the field of Medieval Judaica, but
also as a tribute to a certain aspect of the heroic, perhaps lost to the
modern world.

I owe a debt of graditude to friends and colleagues who have
assisted me in this undertaking at various times and under different
circumstances. First of all I wish to express my gratitude to Dr.
Samuel Belkin, the late president of Yeshiva University, who was my
friend and mentor who inspired me in my scholarly work. I also owe
a debt of gratitude to Rabbis I. Liebschitz and D. Schapiro and to
my colleague Professor B. Z. A. Metzger. Mr. M. Kohn was quite
helpful in the linguistic technicalities of various chapters. Professors
Rachel Wischnitzer and Carol Silver were extremely helpful and
encouraging.

I wish to thank Mr. H. Star, President of the Littaur Foundation in New York, and the Memorial Foundation for Jewish Culture there, for their aid in making available to me two summers of undivided attention to my research.

I greatly appreciate the courtesies extended to me by the staff of the University Library, Hebrew University Jerusalem, by the Curators of the Bodleian Library, Oxford. Also of assistance were the staffs of the Gottesman Library, Yeshiva University, New York, and of the libraries of the Jewish Theological Seminary and Hebrew Union College-Jewish Institute of Religion, both in New York.

Lastly, my heartfelt thanks goes to my family, who were of greatest support from the inception of this work until its publication.

The Jews and the Crusaders

The Hebrew Chronicles of the First and Second Crusades

General Introduction

Four Hebrew chronicles have come down to us that relate what happened to the Jewish communities in Europe that had the misfortune to be on the route of the Crusaders in the eleventh and twelfth centuries. Three of these chronicles, *The Chronicle of Solomon bar Simson, The Chronicle of Rabbi Eliezer bar Nathan,* and *The Narrative of the Old Persecutions,* or *Mainz Anonymous,* describe events that took place during the First Crusade. The fourth, *Sefer Zekhirah (The Book of Remembrance),* by Rabbi Ephraim of Bonn, describes incidents that occurred during the Second Crusade.

THE CRUSADES

The First Crusade

Shortly after the beginning of the First Crusade, Jewish communities in France and along the Rhine became aware of the impact which the sweeping new movement might have upon their lives. The fate of these communities, particularly those located in the Rhineland, was determined by the route and the events of the early phases of the Crusade. For this reason, a brief review of the accepted

3

history and itinerary may serve to promote a fuller comprehension of those moments described in the Hebrew chronicles of the First Crusade.[1]

It is well known that the First Crusade was conceived in November 1095 at the Council of Clermont, where Pope Urban II called upon all Christendom to liberate the Holy Land from Moslem dominion. In December 1095 the northern French Jewish communities dispatched a letter to their Rhenish brethren, perhaps in response to an earlier Crusader attack at Rouen,[2] warning them of the serious threat represented by the rapidly growing movement. Because they heavily bribed the Crusaders, the French Jewish communities were spared for the most part from the direct assaults their coreligionists in Germany were to suffer.

From France, several successive groups of Crusaders moved toward the Rhineland. Peter the Hermit, followed at intervals by the legions of Godfrey of Bouillon, Volkmar, Gottschalk, and Emicho of Leiningen, journeyed eastward up the Rhine. Both Peter and Godfrey were successfully bribed by the Jewish communities in France and the Rhineland; Gottschalk and Volkmar inflicted relatively little damage on the German Jewish communities. Under the leadership of Emicho, however, Crusaders massacred Jews in the Rhineland as well as in several outlying areas, and as they proceeded along their route they became more and more violent, murdering Jews in ever increasing numbers.

An attack at Speyer resulted in the slaying of twelve Jews who refused to convert to Christianity; the rest were saved by the local bishop. In mid-May, Emicho's men attacked the Jewish community at Worms, where they slaughtered five hundred Jews who were under the bishop's special protection. Emicho's arrival in Mainz was greeted by anti-Jewish riots within the barred gates of the city. In the course of these outbursts a Christian was killed, thus further enraging the populace and provoking defiance of Ruthard, archbishop of Mainz. Disobeying the archbishop's orders, Emicho's allies within the city opened the gates to a massive attack in which some thousand Jews were slain. From Mainz the crusaders moved on to Cologne, where Christian acquaintances managed to hide most of the Jews; the archbishop there succeeded in preventing a repetition of the earlier excesses, although the synagogue was burned and several Jews who refused to convert were murdered. Emicho himself then set out for the East, but some of his followers decided to purge the Moselle valley of Jews. This contingent left Emicho's company to ride to Metz, where they killed twenty-two Jews, and thence to Neuss, Wevelinghofen, Eller, and Xanten, where they slew other Jews before dispersing, some to return to their homelands, others to join the larger armies of Crusaders which had set out before them. The incidents in the Rhineland were followed by Volkmar's attacks on the Jews of Prague,[3] many of whom were massacred at the end of June. Just before he entered Hungary, in Ratisbon, Gottschalk massacred those Jews who refused to accede to his demands of conversion. By the end of July 1096, all of the aforementioned groups had left the Rhineland and were advancing eastward to Byzantium.

This is the portion of the First Crusade which the first three chronicles describe. The events themselves are familiar enough to students and historians of the period. What is relatively unknown is the complex of motives which governed both Christian and Jewish behavior in the German portion of the Crusade. Christian antagonism toward the European Jews was not new to Europe, but it had never before materialized in so violent and tragic a form. Old suspicions were fanned to a fatal heat when the religious sentiment of the Crusaders combined with local popular feeling generated by economic factors. In their turn, the Jews of the Rhineland were distrustful of the Crusaders and zealously faithful to their own religion. However much they were initially surprised by the ferocity of anti-Jewish feeling, they came to view their sufferings as a continuum of Biblical history.

The Hebrew chronicles traced the origins of the Crusade to the address of Urban II at Clermont, yet, in accordance with the four Christian accounts of the speech, never named him responsible for the ensuing anti-Jewish persecutions.[4] Nevertheless, the Crusaders were constantly inbued by evangelical preachers with an enthusiasm for liberating the shrines of Jerusalem, and especially the landmarks of the crucifixion. A concentration upon the sufferings of Christ, and therefore upon Jews as his original tormentors, aroused an antagonism toward the Jews which rivaled, if not surpassed, any enmity toward the Moslems, who were the immediate targets of the Crusade.

Immediate and pressing economic motives also spurred Christian animosity toward the Jews of Europe. Because Christianity condemned as usury the taking of any interest for moneylending, this profession fell mainly into Jewish hands. The kings of France and Germany frequently turned to the Jews for aid whenever their nobles failed to supply economic support for royal enterprises. When the king and his nobles enjoyed an economic reconciliation, the Jews fell into royal disfavor. Furthermore, the clergy sometimes offered the Jews special exemptions and permitted them to store their monies in church treasuries, thus evoking the jealousies of the Christian townspeople. Further fuel was added to anti-Jewish feeling when many Crusaders who were landless knights became in part dependent upon monies borrowed from the Jews in order to equip themselves for the costly journey to Jerusalem.[5]

On the eve of the First Crusade, the economic situation in Germany was undoubtedly a strong factor in the shaping of local attitudes toward the Jews. Trade involving native German merchants began to emerge at this time, and, in the course of its growth, inevitably clashed with the established interests of Jewish commerce. The jealousies of the competing burghers were fanned by the anti-Jewish rhetoric accompanying the Crusades. In some cases, the opportunity to mitigate the threat of Jewish competition was provided by the religiously centered attacks of the Crusaders.

Throughout the Hebrew accounts of the First Crusade, we read of the unfailing antagonism of the burghers, who are described as in league with the Crusaders. The chroniclers generally condemn the Rhenish burghers for their treachery, hypocrisy, and opportunism, making frequent mention of their economic motives.

Although the attitudes of the townsmen are described as relatively uniform, the Hebrew chroniclers offer us no definitive conclusion on the positions taken by Rhineland bishops. At times they extended aid, as in the case of the bishop of Speyer; often enough, however, they were tempted by Jewish wealth, extorting what they could and then neglecting the Jews or even leaving them open to Crusader attack, as Bar Simson reports of the bishop of Worms.

Although they did not incite attacks, on the whole they were not prepared to endanger themselves for the benefit of the Jews.

Rulers and bishops alike were caught up in political entanglements, most notably a lay investiture struggle between Henry IV and the Pope. Henry, a noted protector of the Jews, had previously directed two charters of protection to them: one in 1074 to the Worms community, and a later one in 1090 to the Jews of Speyer. When the leaders of the Rhenish communities demanded the emperor's protection against the Crusaders, they requested it on the basis of the earlier privileges, assuming they had been designated to all German Jewry. Although accorded protection in those instances of royal intervention, for the most part the Jews were victims of the times. Henry, his position undermined by the investiture conflict and weakened further by his prolonged absence in Italy, did not have sufficient power to impose order during the chaotic early phases of the Crusade.

The Second Crusade

The Second Crusade, with which the *Sefer Zekhirah (Book of Remembrance)* of Rabbi Ephraim of Bonn deals, was necessitated by the instability of Crusader rule in the Holy Land. On 1 December 1145, following the fall of Edessa, Pope Eugenius III called upon King Louis VII of France and all his faithful subjects to depart for the East. On Christmas, at court in Bourges, Louis announced his intent to take up the Cross. As his vassals showed no enthusiasm over the project, Louis himself decided to postpone definitive action for three months, meanwhile calling upon Bernard of Clairvaux, one of the most influential figures of the time, to assist him in organizing the Crusade.

In March 1146, St. Bernard spoke at Vézelay before a large group which had traveled from all France for the occasion. The sermon is not recorded, but it is known to have engendered great enthusiasm among the assemblage to follow King Louis on a Crusade.

As in 1096, some of the initial ardor created by the movement was directed against the Jews. In France, Peter the Venerable, in assailing the Jews, accused them of commercial dishonesty and requested that their wealth be channeled into the Crusade.[6] In the Rhineland the response was still more hostile. During a tour of preaching throughout Burgundy, Lorraine, and Flanders, Bernard was summoned by the archbishops of Cologne and Mainz to help quell anti-Jewish riots which had broken out in their respective dioceses. A major instigator of these riots was Radulf, a Cistercian monk, who had been preaching anti-Jewish sentiments throughout the Rhineland. Bernard recalled Radulf and condemned the spilling of Jewish blood, but not before large numbers of Jews in the major Rhenish communities had perished.

Despite the initial fervor of the anti-Jewish persecutions, the Jews suffered less in the Second Crusade than in its predecessor. The Second Crusade was better organized and under more active royal and papal leadership than the more popular First Crusade had been; thus the Jews were able to secure a greater measure of protection from the authorities in the Second Crusade than in the First. In addition, the pastoral letters of St. Bernard, forbidding harm to the Jews, were for the most part heeded. although his theological justifications must have been far from pleasing to the people he protected, who were to be spared only in anticipation of future baptism.[7]

THE HEBREW CHRONICLES OF THE FIRST AND SECOND CRUSADES

Most fascinating as a study in historiography is the fact that the three Hebrew chronicles of the First Crusade (namely, those attributed to Bar Simson and Bar Nathan, and the anonymous *Narrative of the Old Persecutions* or *Mainz Anonymous*) are accounts of precisely the same events, though their geographic focus, emphasis upon incidents, and style of presentation differ. The chronicles of Solomon bar Simson and Eliezer bar Nathan concentrate largely upon the events in Mainz and Cologne, dealing only briefly with occurrences in Speyer and Worms, whereas the anonymous chronicle gives priority to the events in Mainz and Worms. Solomon bar Simson's chronicle, the most detailed of the three, is an extremely coherent narrative, despite a few anachronisms. *The Chronicle of Eliezer bar Nathan* is lyrical rather than narrative in tone. More than half the work is heavily liturgical, with long passages of lamentation interspersed between rather brief descriptions of the events—a stylistic bent in character with the author's devotion to liturgical poetry. The *Mainz Anonymous* is highly anecdotal and probes deeply into several incidents omitted, or mentioned only in passing, in the companion chronicles. It is more analytical and selective than either the liturgical Bar Nathan account, or the more methodical narrative of Solomon bar Simson.

Although the *Sefer Zekhirah* of Ephraim of Bonn deals with the Second Crusade, in style and attitude it remains in the tradition of the three earlier chronicles. Ephraim, like his predecessor, Bar Nathan, was greatly concerned with the composition of liturgy, which yields a lyrical quality to his *Sefer Zekhirah*. The very personal and poignant descriptions of incidents are interlaced with formal lamentations. Above all, the document shows us that during the Second Crusade, the Jews of Germany viewed the persecutions, understood their roles, and greeted their agonies in the same spirit as had their forebears during the First Crusade.

Any differences in style and approach are, however, overwhelmed by the shared doctrine, tradition, and cultural source which leave a distinguishing mark on the histories. Despite their individual traits, the chronicles stand as a monument to a set of common beliefs and ancient allegiances, manifested in the language and style, the themes and the attitudes, and the social and psychological responses of the sufferers.

The Language and Style of the Chronicles

The literary influence of the Bible is perhaps the most easily perceptible of the qualities shared by all the chronicles. During the Middle Ages, the Jews of Europe employed the vulgar tongues of their countries in conducting the business of the day. In prayer, study, and writing, they used Hebrew, but since it was not their daily tongue, it remained the static and archaic Hebrew of the Bible and postbiblical literature. Thus, the language and style of the chronicles echo the Bible, the Talmud, and Midrashic literature; yet the chroniclers shaped these literary sources, transmuting phrases, fragments of verse, and other traditional expressions into what amounts to a new stylistic form.[8]

For the Jews of Europe the Crusades represented the Continental re-emergence of an ancient pattern of oppression which was, henceforth, to continue unbroken in European history. Even when the persecutions of the Crusades first descended upon them, they understood them, the chronicles tell us, as a continuum of the endless sufferings which God had chosen them to endure. The Hebrew narrators' view of their people's agony is reflected in the Biblical passages with which they punctuated their works. The citations employed became literary and philosophical commonplaces which were the repeated legacy of the history and literature of the Jews; thus the Hebrew chroniclers used and reused the same Biblical examples and phrases, in a fashion similar to that of their Christian contemporaries.[9]

Like their Christian contemporaries, the medieval Jews believed that they were part of the cosmic patterns first unfolded in the Bible. As adherents to the typological mode of thought, they saw in most events counterparts in Biblical precedents or archetypes. For these reasons, also, the Hebrew chroniclers alluded quite often to the refrains and metaphors of parallel incidents in the Bible. They even seemed, at times, to shape the significance of the historical events of the Crusades to conform to the patterns of martyrdom, sacrifice, persecution, and failure of faith which distinguished those Biblical episodes to which they alluded.

Occasionally in these accounts, the reader is jarred by an awkward archaism which mars the usually smooth flow of the narrative. Such discordant phrases are in part attributable to the infidelity of the various copyists; often enough the scribes, wishing to enhance the narrative with embellishments, introduced errors and irregularities into the work. Despite these intrusions, the historical and literary value of the four Hebrew narratives is great and they occupy an honorable place beside the work of the Christian medieval chroniclers.

Much debate has surrounded the authorship, historical precedence, mutual relationships, and textual problems of the three narratives of the First Crusade. H. Bresslau identified Bar Simson's version as the oldest and most comprehensive of the three. The chronicles, he asserted, were not sequentially oriented, but were, essentially, different descriptions of the same happenings. Furthermore, he placed the authorship of the Mainz version as late as the fourteenth century, for it includes the notorious libel of well-poisoning that gained circulation in that period.[10]

N. Porges contended that such accusations may be found as early as the eleventh century. Nevertheless, Porges also maintained that the first version is the oldest—and that the second version, Bar Nathan's account, though containing errors and extraneous details borrowed from independent sources, is basically an abridgment of the first; the anonymous chronicle, too, is based on the Bar Simson.[11]

I. Elbogen maintained that on the basis of the known manuscripts no definitive conclusion can be provided as to precedence; he accepted the belief, however, that the Bar Nathan and anonymous accounts are derived from the more encompassing Bar Simson, with the possibility of the existence of an even more comprehensive parent version, lost to us, from which our narratives were derived.[12]

On the other hand it has even been asserted that the Bar Simson account, instead of being the earliest, is actually based on the original anonymous *Narrative of the Old Persecutions*, of which only fragments remain today. An argument adduced is that ordinarily medieval narratives which appear fuller and richer of detail are in fact rife with imaginative supplement. According to such a hypothesis, it is suspected that Bar Simson wrote only part of the chronicle attributed to him—the narrative of Eller—and that later writers expanded his account.[13]

THE RESPONSE OF THE JEWS OF EUROPE TO THE CRUSADES

In such a trying period of woe, persecution, and suffering, some incidence of armed self-defense might be expected. In both *The Chronicle of Solomon bar Simson* and the anonymous *Narrative of the Old Persecutions* we hear of children and adults who, under the leadership of R. Kalonymos bar Meshullam, "donned armor and girded themselves with weapons" but nevertheless were "unable to withstand the onslaught of the foe." Solomon bar Simson also notes five hundred warriors who stood against the invading Crusaders in the city of Šla. Interestingly enough, a late medieval Czech tradition

A list of martyrs slain at Mainz on 27 May 1096, appearing in the Mainz Memorial Book (ca. 1250). See S. Salfeld, *Martyrologium des Nürnberger Memorbuches* (Berlin: Leonhard Simion, 1898), pp. 10, 113. (From S. Levi, *Magenza* [Berlin: Menorah, 1927].)

tells of a duke encouraging Jewish resistance at the time of the Crusade, with the Jews slaying two hundred Germans, then taking refuge in a neighboring castle.[14]

On the whole, though, the chronicle accounts of the Jews who fought the Crusaders reflect the typical fate of the self-defender, for, although permitted to bear arms, the Jews lacked the strength to repel the Crusader attacks.[15]

Of acts of retribution per se, in fact there are only two. Rabbi Eliezer bar Nathan and the anonymous chronicler both mention a youth named Simḥa ha-Cohen who, upon being brought to baptism, drew a knife and murdered the nephew of the local bishop. Ephraim of Bonn reports in the Second Crusade the story of two valiant brothers in Carentan who "stood in defense of their own lives and those of their brethren." While making a successful stand against the foe, they were attacked from the rear and slain.[16]

For the most part, however, the Jews did not see their role as that of arms-bearing soldiers. They considered the conflict of Christians and Moslems the Biblically prophesied war of Gog and Magog,[17] heralding the Messianic Age, and their own suffering, the foretold birth pangs of redemption. They believed, for this reason, that the pious and just response to persecution was that of Abraham to God's behest to sacrifice his son, Isaac. In their eyes, obedience to God was synonymous with sacrificial martyrdom. Thus, in most cases, when surrounded by Crusaders, without hope of escape, the Jews determined to die by their own hands rather than submit to the ultimatum of death by the sword or conversion. These acts of self-destruction were likened to the "self-binding," or *'Akedah*, the Biblical reference to Abraham's sacrifice of Isaac, and, by inference, ultimate sacrifice of oneself in martyrdom.[18] As they describe mass suicides, the chroniclers continually refer to Abraham's obedience to God's will. The parallel was, of course, a bitter one. God had intervened to spare Isaac, but the medieval Jews felt that they were called upon to surpass their Biblical forebears by consummating the sacrifice.

In almost every encounter in the chronicles, when the Jews were described as facing a choice between death and conversion, they preferred death.

Divergent though their views were, the Jews and Christians of medieval Europe were, in some sense, chained together by their sufferings and by history itself. If the Crusaders believed that they were messianic instruments advancing the apocalypse and the final redemption, they were as sorely disappointed as their Jewish countrymen who hoped that through the deaths of the martyrs the coming of the Messiah might be hastened.[19]

Like the early Christian encomia of martyrs who gave their lives for their faith, the Jewish dirges of the Crusade era exalted the martyred dead;[20] indeed, to this day, Jewish liturgy commemorates and mourns the persecutions and martyrdoms of the Rhenish communities during the Crusades.[21]

The Chronicle of
Solomon bar Simson

INTRODUCTION

Although it is generally accepted that.*The Chronicle of Solomon bar Simson* is the fullest of the three Hebrew chronicles of the First Crusade, the nature of the sources employed by the chronicler is quite unclear.

In several instances the narrator begins an account in the third person and continues in the first. We do not know what these changes in subject pronoun indicate about the directness or indirectness of the account. In all probability, the chronicle was culled from both eyewitness accounts and secondary sources; all were incorporated without changing the pronouns of the originals.

That Bar Simson himself authored the entire chronicle is dubious. To date our only information about him appears in a paragraph which follows his narrative of Eller. There we read, "Up to this time, in the year [four thousand] nine hundred [1140 C.E.], have I, Solomon bar Simson, recorded this occurrence in Mainz." Quite possibly this passage concluded the only portion of the narrative done by him; all the succeeding accounts perhaps were later additions, as reflected by the use of many Germanisms of a type not found in the Hebrew literature of the twelfth century.

Furthermore, the text that we have of *The Chronicle of Solomon bar Simson* is in all likelihood incomplete. It is generally accepted that a register of martyrs of the three Rhenish communities of Speyer, Worms, and Mainz preceded Bar Simson's narrative.[1]

15

In some sections of the chronicle, both the sources and the infiuences are clear. For example, we may assume that the sections on self-immolation were compiled after the second half of the twelfth century, reflecting the influence of the doctrine of faith and martyrdom of the mystical *Sefer Ḥasidim*. To that same period belong the parts describing the massacres in Mainz, especially those segments in which we are told of dead souls praying for the community in the synagogue of Mainz. Some of the narrator's derogatory references to the Holy Family were clearly influenced by the earlier *Ma'aseh Yeshu* (The Story of Jesus), or *Toldot Yeshu* (The History of Jesus). This work originated during the early centuries of the Church as a Jewish alternative to the life of Christ as portrayed in the Gospels. The advent of the Dark Ages and the increasing resentment born of the rising antipathy of the Church strengthened the bitterness and sarcasm of the caricature. The existence of this work was known to medieval theologians, for although the book itself was kept in secrecy by the Jews, its influence was discernible in many spheres of the Jewish literature of the Middle Ages.

The chronicle begins with a brief account of the persecutions of the Jews of Speyer, Worms, and Mainz, and then proceeds to the main section, a detailed description of the events at Mainz. The chronicler's concern for Mainz was evidently twofold. First, he wrote, according to his testimony, from that city. Second, he maintained that in Mainz more were slain, with fewer converting there than in any of the other Rhenish communities. The narrative continues with descriptions of the events in the towns of Xanten, Mehr, Trier, Regensburg, Prague, and Wesseli (in Bohemia). Evidently, the summary of these events was borrowed from one of the accounts the narrator used. However, having found a more detailed account of Trier, as well as more particulars about Metz, Regensburg, and Wesseli, the chronicler saw nothing inconsistent in adding these after having already summarized his story. The chronicle then concludes with an account of the Crusaders' march through Hungary.

Although many of the events recorded by Solomon bar Simson are borne out by Christian sources, there are some differences. Some of these disparities can be attributed to textual weakness and scribal error. For example, in the invasion of Hungary, Emicho is said to have crossed the border at Innsbruck, a location quite distant from the known route followed by the Crusaders. The reference, in all likelihood is to Wieselburg (near the present-day Magyaróvar, in western Hungary), a location known also as Moson on the Leitha, recorded in Hungarian sources as the place where the Crusaders were bogged down.

In addition, in recounting Peter's passage through Hungary, Bar Simson seems to have enmeshed the accounts of several different groups of Crusaders passing along the same route. At first, in attributing to Peter various previous assaults upon the Hungarians, the chronicler seems to confuse him with later bands, particularly those led by Volkmar and Gottschalk. Guibert of Nogent[2] also attributed to Peter such attacks, perhaps indicating the utilization of sources similar to Bar Simson's. Nevertheless, it is generally accepted that Peter's passage through Hungary was uneventful, encounters with the Hungarians beginning only upon his arrival at Semlin, on the southeast border.[3]

The account reported by Bar Simson of the king's initial warning to the Crusaders (perhaps in response to the unruly behavior of the earlier group led by Volkmar) and of subsequent encounters with the Hungarian peasants well matches the reports of Ekkehard of Aura and Albert of Aix concerning the passage of Gottschalk.[4] Nevertheless, Bar Simson did not remain faithful to the general account of Gottschalk's passage. His group was captured by the Hungarians at Stuhlweissenberg (Székesfehérvár) and annihilated before ever reaching the Danube. Our chronicler knew of Peter's encounters with the Hungarians at Semlin, to the southeast, and thus returned to an account based for the most part on Peter's exploits.

The crossing of the Danube did indeed take place, but no mention is found of the subsequent destruction of a village at that point as reported by Bar Simson. (The author confused the crossing of the Danube with the later crossing of the Save, during which a village was pillaged and "the wood of the houses [was used] as logs.")

Bar Simson's record of the sacking of Semlin substantiates the non-Jewish sources. In particular, the account of the Hungarians' suspicions concerning the size of Peter's army and the ensuing attack and massacre closely parallels Albert of Aix's account.[5] Bar Simson's note of Peter's thirst for vengeance, though not unusual for the

Hebrew chronicler, corresponds to a similar report mentioned by Albert—a surprising corroboration because Peter was usually described in gentile sources as pacific.

At this point, Peter's army fled toward the Save in fear of a Hungarian retaliation for the destruction of Semlin. Nicetas, administering the Byzantine province of Bulgaria at Nish, took measures to restrict the crossing; several of his mercenaries were captured and later executed by the Crusaders.[6] The Crusaders then proceeded directly to Nish.

Bar Simson's account of the destruction of Peter's army at the Save is fallacious; his aim was to emphasize the punishment wreaked upon the Crusaders for massacring the Jewish communities. For this purpose the defeats of the Crusaders were often exaggerated or misrepresented.

Our narrator was in error also about two other points. He refers to Apulia as the residence of the emperor, who actually then resided in northern Italy. Furthermore, the emperor Henry IV spent seven years in Italy (1090–1097), not nine as stated in the chronicle.

Often the chronicler diverges from the Christian sources not in matters which we necessarily accept as facts, but in statistics. For example, the narrator of this chronicle mentions a small number of converts to Christianity during the assault on the Jewish community of Trier. In contrast, the Christian sources report a rather large group of converts, including a certain Rabbi Micah.[7] As often as not, *The Chronicle of Solomon bar Simson* substantiates the Christian sources, as in the report of women and children accompanying the Crusaders,[8] the description of Emicho's viciousness, and the account of Archbishop Ruthard's sympathetic role. Where the differences between Bar Simson's chronicle and those of the Christians are greatest, we feel the bias of a partisan of the Jews. The claim of five hundred warriors defending the community of Šla[9] seems exaggerated. In praising the return of the forced converts at Regensburg, he neglects the fact that they returned to Judaism only in 1097 following Henry's sojourn in Italy. The chronicler even attempts to exonerate the converts of Bavaria and Bohemia by dwelling upon the belief that they endangered themselves by observing Jewish law in secret.

Obviously we must recognize that our chronicler, like any other historian of the period, was not devoted to modern concepts of historical accuracy. Rather, his concern was for revealing a profound scheme which he saw unfolding in the history of his people, their sufferings, and their fulfillment. The chronicler did not conclude his history with the conquest of Jerusalem in late July 1099. Whatever the reason for this missing fact, it is obvious that the narrator did not wish to emphasize the ultimate victory of the Crusaders, but to conclude his tale with their defeat. He dwells upon the triumphant martyrdom of the resistant communities rather than the forced conversion of the others, for his is a history of the glory of virtue and the defeat of evil.

The manuscript serving as the basis for the printed versions of *The Chronicle of Solomon bar Simson* is at the library of Jews' College in London. It is classified as Manuscript code 28, folio 151–63. This copy was written in Treviso in the year 1453 and is the sole copy of which we have knowledge. The full classification is listed in the *Catalogue of the Hebrew Manuscripts in the Jews' College*, compiled by A. Neubauer.[10]

Opening page of the only extant manuscript of *The Chronicle of
Solomon bar Simson*, dating from 1453. This manuscript was copied
from an earlier one. (Courtesy of the Library of Jews' College,
London, and Jewish National and University Library, Jerusalem.)

20

The
Chronicle of
Solomon
bar Simson

I will now recount the event of this persecution in other martyred communities as well—the extent to which they clung to the Lord, God of their fathers, bearing witness to His Oneness to their last breath.[1]

In the year four thousand eight hundred and fifty-six, the year one thousand twenty-eight of our exile,[2] in the eleventh year of the cycle Ranu,[3] the year in which we anticipated salvation and solace, in accordance with the prophecy of Jeremiah: "Sing with gladness for Jacob, and shout at the head of the nations," etc.[4]—this year turned instead to sorrow and groaning, weeping and outcry. Inflicted upon the Jewish People were the many evils related in all the admonitions;[5] those enumerated in Scripture as well as those unwritten were visited upon us.

At this time arrogant people, a people of strange speech, a nation bitter and impetuous, Frenchmen and Germans, set out for the Holy City, which had been desecrated by barbaric nations, there to seek their house of idolatry and banish the Ishmaelites and other denizens of the land and conquer the land for themselves. They decorated themselves prominently with their signs, placing a profane symbol—a horizontal line over a vertical one—on the vestments of every man and woman whose heart yearned to go on the stray path to the grave of their Messiah. Their ranks swelled until the number of men, women, and children[6] exceeded a locust horde covering the earth; of them it was said: "The locusts have no king [yet go they forth all of

21

them by bands] ."[7] Now it came to pass that as they passed through the towns where Jews dwelled, they said to one another: "Look now, we are going a long way to seek out the profane shrine[8] and to avenge ourselves on the Ishmaelites, when here, in our very midst, are the Jews—they whose forefathers murdered and crucified him for no reason.[9] Let us first avenge ourselves on them and exterminate them from among the nations so that the name of Israel will no longer be remembered, or let them adopt our faith and acknowledge the offspring of promiscuity."[10]

When the Jewish communities became aware of their intentions, they resorted to the custom of our ancestors, repentance, prayer, and charity.[11] The hands of the Holy Nation turned faint at this time, their hearts melted, and their strength flagged. They hid in their innermost rooms to escape the swirling sword. They subjected themselves to great endurance, abstaining from food and drink for three consecutive days and nights, and then fasting many days from sunrise to sunset, until their skin was shriveled and dry as wood upon their bones. And they cried out loudly and bitterly to God.

But their Father did not answer them; He obstructed their prayers, concealing Himself in a cloud through which their prayers could not pass, and He abhorred their tent, and He removed them out of His sight—all of this having been decreed by Him to take place "in the day when I visit";[12] and this was the generation that had been chosen by Him to be His portion, for they had the strength and the fortitude to stand in His Sanctuary, and fulfill His word, and sanctify His Great Name in His world. It is of such as these that King David said: "Bless the Lord, ye angels of His, ye almighty in strength, that fulfil His word," etc.[13]

That year, Passover fell on Thursday, and the New Moon[14] of the following month, Iyar, fell on Friday and the Sabbath. On the eighth day of Iyar, on the Sabbath, the foe attacked the community of Speyer and murdered eleven holy souls[15] who sanctified their Creator on the holy Sabbath and refused to defile themselves by adopting the faith of their foe. There was a distinguished, pious woman there who slaughtered herself in sanctification of God's Name. She was the first among all the communities of those who were slaughtered. The remainder were saved by the local bishop[16] without defilement [i.e., baptism] , as described above.[17]

On the twenty-third of Iyar they attacked the community of Worms. The community was then divided into two groups; some remained in their homes and others fled to the local bishop seeking refuge.[18] Those who remained in their homes were set upon by the steppe-wolves who pillaged men, women, and infants, children and old people. They pulled down the stairways and destroyed the houses, looting and plundering; and they took the Torah Scroll, trampled it in the mud, and tore and burned it. The enemy devoured the children of Israel with open maw.

Seven days later, on the New Moon of Sivan[19] —the very day on which the Children of Israel arrived at Mount Sinai to receive the Torah—those Jews who were still in the court of the bishop were subjected to great anguish. The enemy dealt them the same cruelty as the first group and put them to the sword. The Jews, inspired by the valor of their brethren, similarly chose to be slain in order to sanctify the Name before the eyes of all, and exposed their throats for their heads to be severed for the glory of the Creator. There were also those who took their own lives, thus fulfilling the verse: "The mother was dashed in pieces with her children."[20] Fathers fell upon their sons, being slaughtered upon one another, and they slew one another—each man his kin, his wife and children; bridegrooms slew their betrothed, and merciful women their only children. They all accepted the divine decree wholeheartedly and, as they yielded up their souls to the Creator, cried out: "Hear, O Israel, the Lord is our God, the Lord is One." The enemy stripped them naked, dragged them along, and then cast them off, sparing only a small number whom they forcibly baptized in their profane waters. The number of those slain during the two days was approximately eight hundred— and they were all buried naked. It is of these that the Prophet Jeremiah lamented: "They that were brought up in scarlet embrace dunghills."[21] I have already cited their names above.[22] May God remember them for good.

When the saints, the pious ones of the Most High, the holy community of Mainz, whose merit served as shield and protection[23] for all the communities and whose fame had spread throughout the many provinces, heard that some of the community of Speyer had been slain and that the community of Worms had been attacked a second time,[24] and that the sword would soon reach them, their hands became faint and their hearts melted and became as water. They cried out to the Lord with all their hearts, saying: "O Lord, God of Israel, will You completely annihilate the remnant of Israel? Where are all your wonders which our forefathers related to us, saying: 'Did You not bring us up from Egypt and from Babylonia and rescue us on numerous occasions?' How, then, have You now forsaken and abandoned us, O Lord, giving us over into the hands of evil Edom[25] so that they may destroy us? Do not remove Yourself from us, for adversity is almost upon us and there is no one to aid us."

The leaders of the Jews gathered together and discussed various ways of saving themselves. They said: "Let us elect elders so that we may know how to act, for we are consumed by this great evil." The elders decided to ransom the community by generously giving of their money and bribing the various princes and deputies and bishops and governors. Then, the community leaders who were respected by the local bishop[26] approached him and his officers and servants to negotiate this matter. They asked: "What shall we do about the news we have received regarding the slaughter of our brethren in Speyer and Worms?" They [the Gentiles] replied: "Heed our advice and bring all your money into our treasury. You, your wives, and your children, and all your belongings shall come into the courtyard of the bishop until the hordes have passed by. Thus will you be saved from the errant ones."

Actually, they gave this advice so as to herd us together and hold us like fish that are caught in an evil net,[27] and then to turn us over to the enemy, while taking our money. This is what actually happened in the end, and "the outcome is proof of the intentions."[28] The bishop assembled his ministers and courtiers—mighty ministers, the noblest in the land—for the purpose of helping us; for at first it had been his desire to save us with all his might, since we had given him and his ministers and servants a large bribe in return for their promise to help us.[29] Ultimately, however, all the bribes and entreaties were of no avail to protect us on the day of wrath and misfortune.

It was at this time that Duke Godfrey [of Bouillon],[30] may his bones be ground to dust,[31] arose in the hardness of his spirit, driven by a spirit of wantonness to go with those journeying to the profane shrine, vowing to go on this journey only after avenging the blood of the crucified one by shedding Jewish blood and completely eradicating any trace of those bearing the name "Jew," thus assuaging his own burning wrath. To be sure, there arose someone to repair the breach[32] —a God-fearing man who had been bound to the most holy of altars[33] —called Rabbi Kalonymos,[34] the *Parnass* of the community of Mainz.[35] He dispatched a messenger to King Henry[36] in the kingdom of Pula, where the king had been dwelling during the past nine years, and related all that had happened.[37]

The king was enraged and dispatched letters to all the ministers, bishops, and governors of all the provinces of his realm, as well as to Duke Godfrey, containing words of greeting and commanding them to do no bodily harm to the Jews and to provide them with help and refuge.[38] The evil duke then swore that he had never intended to do them harm. The Jews of Cologne nevertheless bribed him with five hundred *zekukim*[39] of silver, as did the Jews of Mainz. The duke assured them of his support and promised them peace.

However, God, the maker of peace, turned aside and averted His eyes from His people, and consigned them to the sword. No prophet, seer, or man of wise heart was able to comprehend how the sin of the people infinite in number was deemed so great as to cause the destruction of so many lives in the various Jewish communities. The martyrs endured the extreme penalty normally inflicted only upon one guilty of murder. Yet, it must be stated with certainty that God is a righteous judge, and we are to blame.

Then the evil waters prevailed.[40] The enemy unjustly accused them of evil acts they did not do, declaring: "You are the children of those who killed our object of veneration, hanging him on a tree;[41] and he himself had said: 'There will yet come a day when my children will come and avenge my blood.'[42] We are his children and it is therefore obligatory for us to avenge him since you are the ones who rebel and disbelieve in him. Your God has never been at peace with you. Although He intended to deal kindly with you, you have conducted yourselves improperly before Him. God has forgotten you and is no longer desirous of you since you are a stubborn nation. Instead, He has departed from you and has taken us for His portion, casting His radiance upon us."[43]

When we heard these words, our hearts trembled and moved out of their places. We were dumb with silence, abiding in darkness, like those long dead, waiting for the Lord to look forth and behold from heaven.

And Satan—the Pope of evil Rome—also came and proclaimed to all the nations[44] believing in that stock of adultery—these are the stock of Seir[45]—that they should assemble and ascend to Jerusalem so as to conquer the city, and journey to the tomb of the superstition whom they call their god. Satan came and mingled with the nations, and they gathered as one man to fulfill the command, coming in great numbers like the grains of sand upon the seashore, the noise of them clamorous as a whirlwind and a storm. When the drops of the bucket had assembled,[46] they took evil counsel against the people of the Lord and said: "Why should we concern ourselves with going to war against the Ishmaelites dwelling about Jerusalem, when in our midst is a people who disrespect our god—indeed, their ancestors are those who crucified him. Why should we let them live and tolerate their dwelling among us? Let us commence by using our swords against them and then proceed upon our stray path."

The heart of the people of our God grew faint and their spirit flagged, for many sore injuries had been inflicted upon them and they had been smitten repeatedly. They now came supplicating to God and fasting, and their hearts melted within them. But the Lord did as He declared, for we had sinned before Him, and He forsook the sanctuary of Shiloh—the Temple-in-Miniature—which He had placed among His people who dwelt in the midst of alien nations.[47] His wrath was kindled and He drew the sword against them, until they remained but as the flagstaff upon the mountaintop and as the ensign on the hill, and He gave over His nation into captivity and trampled them underfoot. See, O Lord, and consider to whom Thou hast done thus: to Israel, a nation despised and pillaged, Your chosen portion! Why have You uplifted the shield of its enemies, and why have they gained in strength? Let all hear, for I cry out in anguish; the ears of all that hear me shall be seared: How has the staff of might been broken, the rod of glory—the sainted community comparable to fine gold, the community of Mainz! It was caused by the Lord to test those that fear Him, to have them endure the yoke of His pure fear.

One day a Gentile woman came, bringing a goose which she had raised since it was newborn. The goose would accompany her wherever she went.[48] The Gentile woman now called out to all passersby: "Look, the goose understands my intention to go straying and desires to accompany me."

At that time, the errant ones gathered against us, and the burghers and peasants said to us: "Where is He in Whom you place your trust? How will you be saved? Now you shall see that these are the wonders which the crucified one works for them [the Crusaders] to signal that they should exact vengeance from their enemies." And they all came with swords to destroy us. But some of the leading burghers stood up to them, and prevented them from harming us.

At this point, the errant ones all united and battled the burghers, and the Gentiles fought with each other, until a Crusader was slain. Seeing this the Crusaders cried out: "The Jews have caused this," and nearly all of them reassembled, reviling and deriding them with the intention of falling upon them.

When the holy people saw this, their hearts melted. Upon hearing their words, the Jews, old and young alike, said: "Would that our death might be by the hands of the Lord, so that we should not perish at the hands of the enemies of the Lord! For He is a Merciful King, the sole sovereign of the universe."

They abandoned their houses; neither did they go to the synagogue save on the Sabbath preceding the month of Sivan—the final Sabbath before the evil decree befell us—when a small number of them entered the synagogue to pray. Rabbi Judah, son of Rabbi Isaac, also came there to pray with that *minyan*.[49] They wept exceedingly, to the point of exhaustion, for they saw that it was a decree of the King of Kings, not to be nullified.

A venerable student, Baruch, son of Isaac, was there, and he said to us: "Know in truth and honesty this decree has been issued against us, and we cannot be saved; for this past night I and my son-in-law Judah heard the souls praying in the synagogue in a loud voice, like weeping.[50] When we heard the sound, we thought at first that perhaps some of the community had come from the court of the bishop to pray in the synagogue at midnight. In our anguish and bitterness of heart we ran to the door of the synagogue to see who was praying. The door was closed. We heard the sound and the loud wailing, but we did not understand a word of what was being said. We returned dismayed to our house—for it was close to the synagogue. Upon hearing this, we cried out: 'Ah Lord God! Wilt Thou make a full end of the remnant of Israel?'"[51] Then they went and reported the occurrence to their brethren who were concealed in the court of the count and in the bishop's chambers, and all knew that this decree was of God. Thereupon, they, too, wept exceedingly, declaring themselves ready to accept God's judgment, saying: "Righteous art Thou, O Lord, and upright are Thy judgments."[52]

On the New Moon of Sivan, Count Emicho,[53] the oppressor of all the Jews—may his bones be ground to dust between iron millstones—arrived outside the city with a mighty horde of errant ones and peasants. They encamped in tents, since the gates of the city were closed, for he, too, had said: "I desire to follow the stray course." He was made leader of the hordes and concocted a tale that an apostle of the crucified one had come to him and made a sign on his flesh[54] to inform him that when he arrived at Magna Graecia,[55] he [Jesus] himself would appear and place the kingly crown upon his head, and Emicho would vanquish his foes. This man was chief of our oppressors. He showed no mercy to the aged, or youths, or maidens, babes or sucklings—not even the sick. And he made the people of the Lord like dust to be trodden underfoot, killing their young men by the sword and disemboweling their pregnant women. They encamped outside the city for two days.

At this time, when the evildoer arrived at Mainz on his way to Jerusalem, the elders of the Jewish community approached their bishop, Ruthard,[56] and bribed him with three hundred *zekukim* of silver. Ruthard had intended to journey to the villages that were subject to the authority of the bishops, but the Jewish community came and bribed and entreated him, until they persuaded him to remain in Mainz, and he took the entire community into his inner chamber, with the words: "I have agreed to aid you." The count, too, declared: "I also wish to remain here in order to help you, but you will have to provide all our needs until those who bear the symbol have passed"; and the community agreed to these terms.

The two of them—the bishop and the count—thereupon acceded to the request of the Jews and said: "We shall die with you or remain alive with you." The community then said: "Since these two who are close to us have granted our request, let us now send our money to the evildoer Emicho, and give him letters of safe conduct so that the communities along the route will honor him.[57] Perhaps the Lord will intercede in His abundant grace and cause him to refrain from his present intentions. It is for this very purpose that we have generously expended our money, giving the bishop, his officers, his servants, and the burghers about four hundred *zekukim* of silver." We dispatched seven pounds of gold to the evil Emicho—so as to aid ourselves, but it was of no avail whatever, and up to the present time we have had no respite from our affliction. We were not even comparable to Sodom and Gomorrah; for in their case they were offered reprieve if they could produce at least ten righteous people, whereas in our case not twenty, not even ten, were sought.[58]

On the third day of Sivan,[59] a day of sanctification and abstinence for Israel in preparation for receiving the Torah, the very day on which our Master Moses, may he rest in peace, said: "Be ready against the third day"[60]—on that very day the community of Mainz, saints of the Most High, withdrew from each other in sanctity and purity, and sanctified themselves to ascend to God all together. Those who had been "pleasant in their lives . . . in their death they were not divided,"[61] for all of them were gathered in the courtyard of the bishop. God's wrath was kindled against His people, and He fulfilled the intention of the errant ones, who succeeded in their purpose; and all our wealth did not avail us, nor did our fasting, self-affliction, lamenting, or charity, and no one was found to stand in the breach[62]—neither teacher nor prince—and even the holy Torah did not shelter its scholars. "And the daughter of Zion was shorn of all her splendor"[63]—this refers to Mainz. Silenced were the voices of the leaders of the flock, "those who wage war,"[64] they that sway the many to righteousness; and silenced was the city of praise, the metropolis of joy, which had generously distributed great sums of money to the poor. An iron stylus writing upon a folio would not suffice to record her numerous good deeds extending back to ancient times—the city in which there were to be found simultaneously Torah and greatness and riches and glory and wisdom and modesty and good deeds, where "prohibition was added upon prohibition"[65] so as to assure scrupulous adherence to the teaching of the Talmud: now this wisdom was completely destroyed, as happened to the dwellers of Jerusalem at the time of its destruction.

At midday the evil Emicho, oppressor of the Jews, came to the gate with his entire horde. The townspeople opened the gate to him,[66] and the enemies of the Lord said to one another: "See, they have opened the gate for us; now let us avenge the blood of the crucified one."

When the people of the Holy Covenant, the saints, the fearers of the Most High, saw the great multitude, a vast horde of them, as the sand upon the seashore, they clung to their Creator. They donned their armor and their wapons of war, adults and children alike, with Rabbi Kalonymos, the son of Rabbi Meshullam, the *Parnass*, at their head.[67] But, as a result of their sufferings and fasts, they did not have the strength to withstand the onslaught of the foe. The troops and legions surged in like a streaming river until finally Mainz was completely overrun from end to end. Emicho had it rumored that the enemy was to be driven from the city,[68] and the Lord's panic was great within the city.

The Jews armed themselves in the inner court of the bishop, and they all advanced toward the gate to fight against the errant ones and the burghers. The two sides fought against each other around the gate, but as a result of their transgressions the enemy overpowered them and captured the gate. The hand of the Lord rested heavily on His people, and all the Gentiles assembled against the Jews in the courtyard to exterminate them. Our people's strength flagged when they saw that the hand of evil Edom was prevailing against them. The bishop's people, who had promised to help them, being as broken reedstaffs, were the first to flee, so as to cause them to fall into the hands of the enemy. The bishop himself fled from his church,[69] for they wanted to kill him, too, because he had spoken in favor of the Jews. The enemy entered the courtyard on the third day of Sivan, the third day of the week—a day of darkness and gloom, a day of clouds and thick darkness; let darkness and the shadow of death claim it for their own. Let God not inquire after it from above, nor let the light shine upon it. Alas for the day on which we saw the torment of our soul! O stars—why did you not withhold your light? Has not Israel been compared to the stars and the twelve constellations, according to the number of Jacob's sons? Why, then, did you not withhold your light from shining for the enemy who sought to eradicate the name of Israel?

When the people of the Sacred Covenant saw that the Heavenly decree had been issued and that the enemy had defeated them and were entering the courtyard, they all cried out together—old and young, maidens and children, menservants and maids—to their Father in Heaven. They wept for themselves and for their lives and proclaimed the justness of the Heavenly judgment, and they said to one another: "Let us be of good courage and bear the yoke of the Holy Creed, for now the enemy can only slay us by the sword, and death by the sword is the lightest of the four deaths.[70] We shall then merit eternal life, and our souls will abide in the Garden of Eden in the presence of the great luminous speculum forever."

All of them declared willingly and wholeheartedly, "After all things, there is no questioning the ways of the Holy One, blessed be He and blessed be His Name, Who has given us His Torah and has commanded us to allow ourselves to be killed and slain in witness to the Oneness of His Holy Name. Happy are we if we fulfill His will, and happy is he who is slain or slaughtered and who dies attesting the Oneness of His Name. Such a one is destined for the World-to-Come, where he will sit in the realm of the saints—Rabbi Akiba and his companions, pillars of the universe, who were killed in witness to His Name.[71] Moreover—for such a one a world of darkness is exchanged for a world of light, a world of sorrow for one of joy, a transitory world for an eternal world."

Then in a great voice they all cried out as one: "We need tarry no longer, for the enemy is already upon us. Let us hasten and offer ourselves as a sacrifice before God. Anyone possessing a knife should examine it to see that it is not defective, and let him then proceed to slaughter us in sanctification of the Unique and Eternal One, then slaying himself—either cutting his throat or thrusting the knife into his stomach."

Upon entering the courtyard, the enemy encountered some of perfect piety, including Rabbi Isaac, son of Rabbi Moses, uprooter of mountains.[72] He extended his neck and was the first to be decapitated. The others wrapped themselves in their fringed prayer shawls and sat in the courtyard waiting to expedite the will of their Creator, not wishing to flee within the chambers just to be saved for temporal life, for lovingly they accepted Heaven's judgment. The foe hurled stones and arrows at them, but they did not scurry to flee; the enemy smote all whom they found there with their swords, causing slaughter and destruction.

Those Jews in the chambers, seeing what the enemy had inflicted upon the saints, all cried out: "There is none like our God unto whom it would be better to offer our lives." The women girded their loins with strength and slew their own sons and daughters, and then themselves. Many men also mustered their strength and slaughtered their wives and children and infants. The most gentle and tender of women slaughtered the child of her delight. They all arose, man and woman alike, and slew one another. The young maidens, the brides, and the bridegrooms looked out through the windows and cried out in a great voice: "Look and behold, O Lord, what we are doing to sanctify Thy Great Name, in order not to exchange You for a crucified scion who was despised, abominated, and held in contempt in his own generation, a bastard son conceived by a menstruating and wanton mother."[73]

Thus the precious children of Zion, the people of Mainz, were tested with ten trials as was our Father Abraham,[74] and as Ḥananiah, Mishael, and Azariah were.[75] They, too, bound[76] their children in sacrifice, as Abraham did his son Isaac, and willingly accepted upon themselves the yoke of fear of Heaven, of the King of Kings, the Blessed Holy One. Refusing to gainsay their faith and replace the fear of our King with an abominable stock, bastard son of a menstruating and wanton mother, they extended their necks for slaughter and offered up their pure souls to their Father in Heaven. The saintly and pious women acted in a similar manner, extending their necks to each other in willing sacrifice in witness to the Oneness of God's Name—and each man likewise to his son and brother, brother to sister, mother to son and daughter, neighbor to neighbor and friend, bridegroom to bride, fiancé to his betrothed: each first sacrificed the other and then in turn yielded to be sacrificed, until the streams of blood touched and mingled, and the blood of husbands joined with that of their wives, the blood of fathers with that of their sons, the blood of brothers with that of their sisters, the blood of teachers with that of their pupils, the blood of bridegrooms with that of their brides, the blood of community deacons with that of their scribes, the blood of babes and sucklings with that of their mothers—all killed and slaughtered in witness to the Oneness of the Venerated and Awesome Name.

Let the ears hearing this and its like be seared, for who has heard or seen the likes of it? Inquire and seek: was there ever such a mass sacrificial offering since the time of Adam? Did it ever occur that there were one thousand and one hundred offerings on one single day—all of them comparable to the sacrifice of Isaac, the son of Abraham? The earth tembled over just one offering that occurred on the myrrh mountain—it is said: "Behold, the valiant ones cry without,"[77] and the heavens are darkened. What have they [the martyrs] done? Why did the heavens not darken and the stars not withhold their radiance, why did not the sun and the moon turn dark?[78] On a single day—the third of Sivan, the third day of the week—one thousand and one hundred[79] holy souls were killed and slaughtered, babes and sucklings who had not sinned or transgressed, the souls of innocent poor people. Wilt Thou restrain Thyself for these things, O Lord? It was for You that innumerable souls were killed! May You avenge the spilt blood of your servants, in our days and before our very eyes—Amen—and speedily!

That day the diadem of Israel fell, the students of the Torah fell, and the outstanding scholars passed away. The glory of the Torah fell, as it is written: "He hath cast down from heaven unto the earth the splendor of Israel."[80] Gone were the sin-fearers, gone were the men of virtuous deed; ended were the radiance of wisdom and purity and abstinence; [ended was] the glory of the priesthood and of the men of perfect faith—repairers of the breach, nullifiers of evil decrees, and placaters of the wrath of their Creator; diminished were the ranks of those who give charity in secret.[81] Gone was truth; gone were the explicators of the Word and the Law; fallen were the people of eminence and the sage—all on this day, on which so many sorrows befell us and we could turn neither to the right nor to the left from the fury of the oppressor. For since the day on which the Second Temple was destroyed, their like had not arisen, nor shall there be their like again—for they sanctified and bore witness to the Oneness of God's Name with all their heart and with all their soul and with all their might. Happy are they and happy is their lot, for all of them are destined for eternal life in the World-to-Come—and may my place be amongst them!

"And He hath multiplied in the daughter of Judah mourning and moaning."[82] The enemy arose against them, killing little children and women, youth and old men—all on one day. The priests were not accorded honor nor the elders grace; the enemy showed no mercy for babes and sucklings, no pity for women about to give birth. They left no survivor but a dried date and two or three pits.[83] For all of them had been eager to sanctify the Name of their Creator. And when the enemy was upon them, they all cried out in a great voice, with one heart and one tongue: "Hear, O Israel: the Lord our God, the Lord is One."[84]

There was a saintly and pious man there, one of the great men of the generation, Rabbi Menaḥem, the son of Rabbi Judah,[85] who spoke and exhorted his fellow Jews. He cited the words of our Father Jacob, who, just before he died, wished to reveal the time of the Final Redemption to his children, but was prevented from doing so because the Divine Presence[86] departed from him: "Jacob then said: 'Just as our Father Isaac produced a defect, so perhaps I, too, have been found to have a defect.'[87] Whereupon Jacob's sons all answered: 'Hear, O Israel, the Lord is our God, the Lord is One.' And when our fathers received the Torah on Mount Sinai at this season, they said: 'We shall do and obey,'[88] and declared in a great voice: 'Hear, O Israel, the Lord is our God, the Lord is One.' Thus shall you do this day." and they wholeheartedly affirmed the Oneness of God, doing as the great sage had told them, crying out with one mouth and one heart: "Hear, O Israel, the Lord is our God, the Lord is One." At this time, Rabbi Isaac, son of Rabbi Moses, and the other prominent rabbis were gathered in the courtyard of the bishop—weeping, with their necks outstretched, and saying: "When will the pillager come, so that we may receive Heaven's judgment? We have already arranged the offerings and prepared the altars in His Name."

I will now tell and relate the great wonders which were performed that very day by these saints. Let one and all behold—has the like of this ever occurred? For they all vied with one another, each with his fellow, saying: "I shall be the first to sanctify the Name of the Supreme King of Kings—the Blessed Holy One." In addition, the saintly women, daughters of kings, would cast coins and silver out through the windows to the enemy, so that they would be preoccupied with gathering the money and thus tarry while the women finished slaughtering their sons and daughters. The hands of merciful women slaughtered their children, in order to do the will of their Creator. The enemy came into the chambers, they smashed the doors, and found the Jews still writhing and rolling in blood; and the enemy took their money, stripped them naked, and slew those still alive, leaving neither a vestige nor a remnant. Thus they did in all the chambers where children of the Sacred Covenent were to be found. But one room remained which was somewhat difficult to break into; there the enemy fought till nightfall.

When the saints saw that the enemy was prevailing over them and that they would be unable to withstand them any longer, they acted speedily; they rose up, men and women alike, slaughtered the children. Then the righteous women hurled stones from the windows on the enemy, and the enemy threw rocks back at them. The women were struck by the stones, and their bodies and faces were completely bruised and cut. They taunted and reviled the errant ones with the name of the crucified, despicable, and abominable son of harlotry, saying: "In whom do you place your trust? In a putrid corpse!" The misled ones then approached to smash the door.

Who has seen or heard of an act like the deed of the righteous and pious young Mistress Rachel, daughter of Isaac, son of Asher, and wife of Judah? She said to her friends: "Four children have I. Have no mercy on them either, lest those uncircumcised ones come and seize them alive and raise them in their ways of error.[89] In my children, too, shall you sanctify the Holy Name of God." One of her friends came and took the knife to slaughter her son. When the "mother of the sons" saw the knife,[90] she cried loudly and bitterly and smote her face and breast, and said: "Where is Your grace, O Lord?" With an embittered heart she [the mother] said to her companions: "Do not slaughter Isaac before his brother Aaron, so that he [Aaron] will not see the death of his brother and flee." A friend took the boy and slew him. A delightful little child he was. The mother spread her sleeves to receive the blood, according to the practice in the ancient Temple sacrificial rite.[91] The lad Aaron, upon seeing that his brother had been slaughtered, cried: "Mother, do not slaughter me," and fled, hiding under a box.

She also had left two daughters, Bella and Madrona, modest and beautiful maidens. The maidens took the knife and sharpened it, so that it would have no notch. They extended their throats, and the mother sacrificed them to the Lord, God of Hosts, Who commanded us not to depart from His pure doctrine, and to remain wholehearted with Him, as it is written: "Thou shalt be wholehearted with the Lord thy God."[92]

When this pious woman had completed sacrificing her three children to their Creator, she raised her voice and called to her son: "Aaron, Aaron, where are you? I will not spare you either, or have mercy on you." She drew him out by his feet from under the box where he had hidden and slaughtered him before the Exalted and Lofty God. Then she placed them all on her arms, two children on one side and two on the other, beside her stomach, and they quivered beside her, until finally the enemy captured the chamber and found her there sitting and lamenting over them. They said to her: "Show us the money you have in your sleeves"; but when they saw the slaughtered children, they smote and killed her upon them, and her pure soul expired.

It is of her that it was said: "The mother was dashed in pieces with her children."[93]

Thus she died together with her four children, just as did that other righteous woman with her seven sons,[94] and about them it is written: "The mother of the sons rejoices."[95] When the father saw the death of his four children, beautiful in form and appearance, he cried bitterly and threw himself on the sword in his hand, and was thus disemboweled. He writhed in his blood on the road together with the others quivering and writhing in their blood. The enemy slew all who remained inside and stripped them naked. "See, O Lord, and behold, how abject I am become."[96]

The errant ones then began to rage tumultuously in the name of the crucified one, having their way with all those found in the chamber of the bishop; and there was not a single survivor. They raised their banners, and in an uproar proceeded to the remainder of the community in front of the count's courtyard. They besieged them, too, until they had taken the gatehouse of the courtyard, and slew those who were there.

A saintly man, Moses, son of Ḥelbo, was there. He called his two sons and said to them: "My sons, Ḥelbo and Simon, at this hour Gehenna and the Garden of Eden are both open. Which of the two do you now desire to enter?" They replied, saying: "It is our desire to enter the Garden of Eden." They extended their throats, and the enemy smote them—father and sons together. May their souls be in the Garden of Eden, in the light of life.

There was also a Torah Scroll in the room; the errant ones came into the room, found it, and tore it to shreds. When the holy and pure women, daughters of kings, saw that the Torah had been torn, they called in a loud voice to their husbands: "Look, see, the Holy Torah—it is being torn by the enemy!" And all the women said, in one voice: "Alas, the Holy Torah, the perfection of beauty, the delight of our eyes, to which we used to bow in the synagogue, honoring it; our little children would kiss it. How has it now fallen into the hands of these impure uncircumcised ones?"

When the men heard the words of these pious women, they were moved with zeal for the Lord, our God, and for His holy and precious Torah. A young man by the name of David, son of our master Rabbi Menaḥem, said to them: "My brothers, rend your garments for the honor of the Torah!"[97] They then rent their garments.

They found one of the errant ones in the room, and all of them, men and women, threw stones at him till he fell dead. When the burghers and the errant ones saw that he had died, they fought against them; they went up on the roof of the house in which the children of the Sacred Covenant were; they shattered the roof, shot arrows at them, and hurled objects at them, and pierced them till they were completely annihilated.

There was a very good man there by the name of Jacob, son of Sullam, who was not of distinguished lineage, and whose mother was not of Jewish origin. He called out in a loud voice to all those that stood about him, saying: "Until now you have scorned me. Now see what I shall do." And he took the knife which he was holding in his hand and thrust it into his neck in front of all, and he slaughtered himself in the name of the Mighty of Mighties,[98] Whose Name is Lord of Hosts.

Another man was there, Samuel, son of Mordecai, the Elder. He, too, sanctified the Name. He called to all those standing about him and declared: "Behold, my brothers, what I shall do this day for the sanctification of the Eternally Living One." He took his knife and plunged it into his stomach, spilling his innards onto the ground. Thus did the elder perish in holiness attesting the Oneness of God's Name, sanctifying Godfear.

The errant ones and the burghers departed from there. Puffed up over having had their way with their adversaries, they entered the city, and they came to a certain courtyard. Hidden in the courtyard of a priest were David, son of Nathaniel, the *Gabbai*,[99] his wife, children, and his entire household. The priest said to the members of the family: "Behold, not a vestige or remnant has survived either in the bishop's courtyard and castles or in the count's courtyard. They have all been slain, cast away, and trampled underfoot like the mud of the streets, except for the few who were profaned and who have gone over to their belief. Do as they did, so that you may be saved— you, your money, and your entire household—from the errant ones."

The God-fearing man replied: "Go outside to the errant ones and to the burghers and tell them all, in my name, to come to me." When the priest heard the words of this saintly man, Master David the *Gabbai*, he rejoiced greatly, for he thought: "Such a distinguished Jew has consented to give heed to our words." He ran to those outside and related the words of the righteous man who had sent him. They, too, rejoiced greatly and gathered around the house by the thousands and myriads. When the righteous man saw them, he placed his trust in the God of his fathers and called out to them, saying: "You are children of whoredom, believing as you do in a god who was a bastard and was crucified. As for me—I believe in the Everlasting God Who dwells in the lofty heavens. In Him have I trusted to this day, and I will continue to do so until my soul departs. Moreover, I know the truth: If you slay me, my soul will abide in the Garden of Eden—in the light of life. You, however, descend to the deep pit, to eternal obloquy. To Gehenna are you and your whoreson god condemned, and to boiling excrement will you be consigned."[100]

Upon hearing the words of the pious man reviling them and revealing their shame to them, they flew into a rage. They raised their banners and encamped around the house and began to cry out and shout in the name of the crucified one. They advanced toward him and slew him, his pious wife, his son, his daughter, his son-in-law, and his entire household and his maidservant—all of them were slain in sanctification of the Name. There the righteous man fell together with the members of his household. The mob then threw them out of the windows into the street.

The burghers and the errant ones then turned from there and came to another house—that of Samuel, son of Naaman; he, too, sanctified the Holy Name. They gathered around his house, for he and a few others who had remained with him in his home were the sole survivors of the entire community. They asked him to allow himself to be defiled with their putrid waters. They all refused, placing their trust in the Creator. The enemy slew them all and trampled them underfoot.

For these do I weep and my eyes run with water, for the burning of the sanctuary of our God, and for the death by fire of Isaac, son of David, the *Parnass*, who was consumed by flames in his home.

I shall now tell one and all how this thing happened. On the fifth day of the month of Sivan, the Eve of Pentecost,[101] two saintly men—Master Isaac, the pious, son of David, the *Parnass*, and Uri, son of Joseph—acknowledged their Creator and greatly santified the Name of their Maker.[102] For on the third day, when the entire community had been wiped out, these two pious men had been spared for Hell, as the enemy had defiled them against their will.[103] They therefore now accepted upon themselves a fearful death not recorded in any of the admonitions.

Isaac entered his father's house to see the hidden treasure concealed since the days of his father. He went into the cellar and found that the enemy had left it untouched. He thought: "Of what worth is all this money to me now that the enemy have achieved their design of removing me from the people of the Lord and causing me to have rebelled against God's Holy Torah? What is more, a priest invited me to partake of a repast with him. Do I have any right to this money now? After all, when a man goes to his eternal abode, he is accompanied by neither silver nor gold, but only by repentance and good deeds. I shall therefore repent and be whole of heart with the Lord, God of Israel, until I surrender my soul to Him and yield myself up into His hands. Perhaps He will deal graciously with me so that I may yet be reunited with my companions and be admitted to their company in the precincts of the Great Light. It is well known to Him Who scrutinizes human hearts that I acquiesced to the enemy's demand only in order to save my children from the offspring of iniquity, that they should not be educated in their erring ways, for they are young and unable to distinguish between good and evil."

He went to his father's house and hired laborers to repair the doors of the house, which had been smashed by the enemy. On the fifth day of Sivan, when they had finished, he came to his mother and related his intentions to her. He exclaimed to her: "Mother, I have decided to bring a sin-offering to God of Heaven. Perhaps I will thereby achieve atonement!" The mother, upon hearing the words of her God-fearing son, adjured him not to do this thing. For she overflowed with compassion for him, he being the sole survivor of all her loved ones. His sainted wife, Mistress Skolester, had been slain— she was a daughter of Samuel the Great. The mother herself was bedridden because the enemy had inflicted many wounds on her. Her son Isaac had saved her from death without her having to defile herself, though he himself had been defiled.

Isaac, her saintly son, did not give heed to his mother's pleas. He locked all the doors, with himself, his children, and his mother inside. The pious man then asked his children, "Do you wish me to offer you as a sacrifice to our God?" They replied, "Do as you will with us." The saint then said: "My children, my children, our God is the true God—there is none other!" Master Isaac the saint then took his two children—his son and his daughter—and led them through the courtyard at midnight into the synagogue before the Holy Ark, and there he slaughtered them, in sanctification of the Great Name, to the Sublime and Lofty God, Who has commanded us not to forsake pure fear of Him for any other belief, and to adhere to His Holy Torah with all our heart and soul. He sprinkled some of their blood on the pillars of the Holy Ark[104] so as to evoke their memory before the One-and-Only Everlasting King. And he said: "May this blood expiate all my transgressions!" The pious man now returned by way of the courtyard to his father's house and set the house aflame at its four corners, and his mother, who had remained in the house, was burned in sanctification of God's Name. The pious Master Isaac returned to the synagogue to set it aflame, and he kindled the fire at all the doors. He went from corner to corner, his hands outspread Heavenward–to his Father in Heaven–praying to God out of the flames in a loud and sweet voice. The enemy shouted at him through the windows: "Wicked man, escape the flame; you can still save yourself." They extended a pole toward him in order to draw him from the flames, but the saintly man did not want to grasp it, and died in the flame, an innocent, just, and God-fearing man. And his soul has found shelter in the precincts of righteousness in the Garden of Eden.

Master Uri, too, was involved in the plan to burn the synagogue, for they had heard that the enemy intended to erect either a house of idolatry or a mint on the site. When Isaac set his father's house and the synagogue aflame, Uri was in another house. He had wanted to aid Isaac in the burning of the synagogue, and to be consumed in the conflagration, so that they would thus sanctify the Name of God together. However, he was unable to reach him because the enemy, awakened in the middle of the night by the flames, apprehended and slew him before he reached the fire. Master Isaac was, however, consumed in the flames.

Thus they both fell before God, with one accord, wholeheartedly, for the sake of the Name of Him Who is called [Lord of] Hosts. And it is of them and their like that it is written: "He who offers the sacrifice of thanksgiving honors Me."[105] Some are of the opinion that the forced converts had heard of plans to convert the synagogue into a mint, and that is why the pious man set it afire–himself perishing in the blaze. Others say they heard that the enemy intended to convert the synagogue into a church, and that is why they burnt it.[106]

The majority of the rabbis in all the communities and many distinguished personalities passed away a year before the advent of the day of the Lord, the time of the enactment of the decree. Our master Rabbi Eleazar[107] also passed away then. Thus was fulfilled the verse: "The righteous is taken away from the evil to come."[108]

There were also many women there who sanctified the Name of their Creator to their last breath, not giving Him up for the crucified bastard. One of them was Mistress Rachel, the spouse of our late master, Rabbi Eleazar, who had been the colleague of Rabbi Judah, son of Rabbi Isaac; Rabbi Judah, a famed scholar, had also been slain in sanctification of God's Name. There were other saintly women with them who also sanctified God's Name. These pure souls were brought before the churchyard, where the enemy attempted to persuade them to submit to baptism. When they arrived at the temple of their pagan cult, the women refused to enter the edifice of idolatry, rooting their feet on the threshold, unwilling to enter and inhale the odor of the offensive incense. When the errant ones saw that the women stood firm against the abomination, and, what is more, that they remained true with all their heart to the living God, they fell upon them with axes and smote them. Thus the saintly women were slain in sanctification of God's Name.

There were two other pious women: Mistress Guta, wife of our master, Rabbi Isaac, son of Rabbi Moses, who had been slain earlier, and Mistress Skolester, the wife of Isaac, who had perished in the flames in sanctification of God's Name. These women also sanctified the Name of the Holy One, the Only One, Whose Oneness is on the lips of all living creatures, at the time that the martyred men were slain in the courtyard of the bishop. The women had found sanctuary in the courtyard of a burgher, and the enemy came and drove them from the house, and the errant ones and the burghers surrounded them and demanded that they defile themselves with their evil water. But the women placed their trust in the Holy One of Israel and extended their throats, and the errant ones slew them without mercy. There the saintly women were slain in sanctification of God's One and Venerated Name.

Samuel, son of Isaac, son of Samuel, also sanctified God's Name. He had hidden himself in a certain home, but when he was informed that the martyrs had been slain, he fled from the city to seek refuge with the community of Speyer. The enemy apprehended him and declared: "If you are willing to defile yourself, well and good; otherwise, we shall slit your throat right here and now."

Master Samuel remained silent, not uttering a word, but submitting to God's judgment, and he thereupon extended his throat and they slit it. There the pious man fell in sanctification of the Name, and attested the Oneness of our God, Who is the Holy God. After the children of the Holy Covenant who were in the chambers had been slain, the uncircumcised ones came upon them to strip the fallen bodies and remove them from the rooms. They threw them, naked, through the windows onto the ground, creating mounds upon mounds, heaps upon heaps, until they appeared as a high mountain. Many of them, as they were thrown, still had a breath of life in them, and they gestured with their fingers: "Give us water to drink." When the errant ones saw that there was still some life in them, they asked: "If you are willing to defile yourselves we will give you water to drink and you will be saved." The victims shook their heads in refusal and gazed upward to their Father in Heaven, thus saying no, and pointed with their fingers up at the Blessed Holy One but were unable to utter a sound because of the many wounds that had been inflicted upon them. The enemy continued to smite them, again and again, as if to slay their victims a second time.

Such were the deeds of those whom we have cited by name, deeds which they performed in preparation for the Heavenward journey.[109] As for the rest of the community and their leaders whose deeds and piety have not been enumerated—how much more did they do in attesting the Oneness of the Name of the King of Kings, the Blessed Holy One, like Rabbi Akiba and his companions,[110] undergoing a trial like the one endured by Hananiah, Mishael, and Azariah. They were the subjects of a miracle like the one brought to pass for the fallen of the city of Betar, for whom Talmudic Sages promulgated a regulation that the blessing "He Who is good and acts kindly" should be added to the Grace-after-Meals in memory of the martyrs of Betar—"is good," in that their bodies did not putrefy, and "acts kindly," in gratitude for their ultimate burial.[111] A similar miracle occurred to those saints and pious people, for the burghers buried them using the money which the victims had entrusted to them. But they were buried naked. The burghers dug nine pits in the graveyard and buried young and old together, men with women, fathers with sons, daughters with mothers, servants with masters, maidservants with mistresses—all were hurled one upon the other and were buried there in this manner.

May God-on-High remember them and avenge them speedily in our days. It is of them that it was said: "He will judge among the nations; He filleth it with dead bodies, He crusheth the head over a wide land."[112] And it was further said: "God of vengeance, O Lord, God of vengeance, shine forth!"[113] The murderers are marked for eternal obloquy; those murdered in sanctification of the Holy Name of the Most High God are destined for eternal life and their souls will be bound in Paradise in the bond of life—Amen.

I shall now tell of the murder of Rabbi Kalonymos the Pious, the *Parnass*, and his associates. May God avenge him speedily in our days!

On the very day that the Lord had said to His people, "Be prepared for the third day,"[114] on that day they prepared themselves, extended their throats, and offered up their sacrifice, a sweet savor unto the Lord. On that day eleven hundred[115] holy souls were slain for the sake of the Great Name of Him Who is One in the world, besides Whom there is no god. Only Rabbi Kalonymos, the *Parnass*, the saintly, and fifty-three Jewish youths were saved, fleeing via the bishop's chamber. They came to the vestry in the church, a storage room which is called the sacristy.[116] They remained there in straitened conditions because of the threatening sword. The door of the vestry was narrow, and it was dark, so that none of the enemy noticed them, and they did not breathe a sound.

The sun had set and there was thick darkness; they cried out in distress, and their tongues clung to their palates from thirst. They approached the window and spoke to the sacristan, requesting that he give them water so as to revive themselves, but he refused. They finally gave him ten *zekukim* of silver for a flask full of water, thus fulfilling the Biblical verse, "You shall serve your enemy . . . in hunger and in thirst," etc.[117] He brought the flask to the window, but was unable to hand it to them because the opening was too narrow. Finally he brought a lead pipe through which he passed the water, and they drank moderately, but did not quench their thirst.

I shall now relate the circumstances regarding the slaying of these saints.

At midnight, the bishop sent someone to the window of the vestry to Rabbi Kalonymos, the *Parnass.*[118] He called to him and said: "Hear me, Kalonymos, the bishop has sent me to inquire whether you are still alive, and if so to rescue you and all who are with you. Come out to the bishop, for there are three hundred mailed warriors with drawn swords accompanying him. We are willing to die in your stead. If you do not believe me, I swear to you that my lord the bishop has thus commanded me. He is not in town at present, for he has gone to the village of Rüdesheim, but he has sent me here to rescue those of you who have survived, for the bishop desires to aid you."

The Jews did not believe him till he swore to them. Then Rabbi Kalonymos and his associates came out to him. He provided boats for them, took them across the Rhine River, and brought them to the bishop in the village of Rüdesheim. The bishop was very happy to see that Rabbi Kalonymos was still alive, and promised to save him and those with him.[119] But God had caused the sword of the enemy to be drawn against them, and He did not turn His wrath away from them. He in Whose hand are the watercourses and the hearts of kings and princes had initially turned the bishop's heart favorably toward them [the Jews]. But then the bishop went back on his word. He summoned Rabbi Kalonymos and said: "I cannot save you, for your God has turned away from you and does not wish to allow any of your group to survive. From now on it is no longer in my power to save or help you; now you and your associates must choose between accepting our faith and paying for the iniquity of your forefathers."

The pious Rabbi Kalonymos replied to him, crying out bitterly: "Indeed, it is not our God's wish to save us. Therefore, what you say is true, that it is no longer in your power to save us. But give us until tomorrow to reply to your words." Rabbi Kalonymos then returned to his saintly associates and told them what the bishop had said. They rose as one man, and with one tongue and one heart pronounced a benediction of martyrdom, acknowledged the justness of God's judgment, and accepted upon themselves the yoke of fear of God.

Before returning to the bishop, Rabbi Kalonymos first took his son Joseph, kissed him, and then slew him. When the bishop heard of this, he declared in a great rage: "Now I most certainly do not desire to save you!" When the bishop's words reached the villagers, they and the errant ones gathered to slay the Jews. On that very day, Rabbi Kalonymos set out to go to the bishop, and on his way he learned what the bishop had said. When he reached the bishop, Rabbi Kalonymos had a knife on his person, with the intention of slaying him. The bishop and his men became aware of this, and the bishop ordered Rabbi Kalonymos removed from his presence. The bishop's servants then fell upon him and slew him with a wooden pole.

Another version stated that he did not return to the bishop, but that immediately after slaying his son, he placed his sword, blade up, in the ground, and fell upon it, thus impaling himself on it. Yet another account states that the enemy killed him on his way to the bishop. Whatever the facts about his death, this we know with certainty—that the Exilarch was slain bearing witness to the Oneness of the Name of the King of Kings, the Blessed Holy One, and that he was perfect and wholehearted with the Lord God of Israel; and there the saint fell, slain together with his congregation.

Rabbi Judah, son of our master Rabbi Isaac, and his uncle Isaac, son of Asher, as well as many daughters of Israel, were also slain; all slain and slaughtered in witness to the Oneness of the Name of the God of Israel.

The following were amongst this second group: Shneur; Rabbi Kalonymos, son of Rabbi Joseph the Elder, of Speyer; Isaac, son of Samuel; Isaac, son of Moses; Eliezer, son of Jacob; Ḥelbo, son of Moses; and many others with them—all of them, too, placing their trust in the Rock of Israel. And Shneur had slain one Gentile. The villagers gathered against them in the forest, where the bishop had driven them, and they threw stones and shot arrows, and stabbed them, and slew them by the sword until the mighty ones of Israel fell there; all this was caused by the hand of the Lord. "Wilt Thou restrain Thyself for these things, O Lord?"[120]

Also in that second group at one site in the forest were Abraham, son of Asher, and Samuel, son of Tamar, and many others who also sanctified the Great Supreme God. The enemies now gathered against Abraham, son of Asher, and asked him to defile himself in the evil waters, for he was a well-known and well-loved man. Some of his acquaintances stood near him, and he now said to them: "Is there any man who knows whether a single member of my household or a single one of my children survives?" They replied: "We do not know." The enemy, meanwhile, exhorted him vigorously to defile himself. And he replied to them, saying: "Why do you tarry so long? Upon your lives—slay me, for I shall not acquiesce in this matter; I shall place my trust in the Living God and cling to Him until I yield my soul up to Him." So also did Samuel declare to Abraham: "I shall be with you in life and in death."

The enemy then slew them, for they did not desire to hear their words. They smote Abraham, who fell to the ground and expired; Samuel was also slain there with him. They placed their trust in the Holy One of Israel and they both entered into God's encompassing sanctuary, there to remain till the day of reckoning for the spilt blood of His servants. Then God "will judge among the nations, He filleth it with dead bodies. He crusheth the head over a wide land."[121] And the Scriptures further state: "Sing aloud, O ye nations of His people; for He doth avenge the blood of His servants [and doth render vengeance to His adversaries, and doth make expiation for the land of His people]."[122]

The enemy also slew Rabbi Yekuthiel, son of Rabbi Meshullam, and his son-in-law on the road between Mainz and Rüdesheim, as they returned from the site where his brother, Rabbi Kalonymos, the *Parnass*, had been slain. They had intended to return to the city of Mainz so that they enemy would kill them there, and thus they would be buried in the same cemetery with their brothers who had been saintly, upright, and whole with God. But they did not manage to reach their destination, because the abhorrent ones met and killed them on the way back. Behold, their souls are bound in the bond of eternal life with the Lord our God.

He Who spoke causing the world to come into being—He shall avenge the spilt blood of His servants. The enemy said: "Let us take to ourselves possession of the habitations of God,"[123] and "Let us cut them off from being a nation; that the name of Israel may be no more in remembrance."[124] Our adversaries thought: "The Lord will not see, neither will the God of Jacob give heed."[125]

"God of vengeance, O Lord, God of vengeance, shine forth!"[126]
"For Thy sake are we killed all the day."[127] "And they devour Israel
with open mouth."[128] "See, O Lord, and consider to whom Thou
hast done thus!" Women kill their offspring, their fondled sucklings.
"The youth and the old man lie on the ground in the streets; my
virgins and my young men are fallen by the sword."[129] They
slaughtered in the day of Your anger; they killed and their eyes had
no mercy on us. "Render unto our neighbors sevenfold into their
bosom."[130] "Exalt Thyself, Thou Judge of all the Earth; render [to
the proud] their recompense."[131] And on the enemies of Israel—
raise Thy wrath and wreak Thy vengenance, as it is said: "[They
come from a far country, from the end of heaven, even] The Lord,
and the weapons of His indignation, to destroy the whole earth."[132]
Subsequently, "He will cry, yea, He will shout aloud. He will prove
Himself mighty against His enemies."[133] "Pour out Thy wrath upon
the nations that know Thee not, and upon the kingdoms that call
not upon Thy Name."[134]

"Pour out thine indignation upon them [and let the fierceness
of Thine anger overtake them]."[135] Exact from them the blood of
your servants which was set upon the hard rock.[136]

O Earth, cover not their blood, and let there be no resting place
for our cries! May the Lord, our God, grant us revenge: "Let the
avenging of Thy servants' spilt blood be made known among the
nations in our sight,"[137] speedily, for the sake of Thy Great Name
which we bear. Let all creatures know and understand their iniquity
and guilt for that which they have done to us. Accord unto them as
they have accorded unto us.

Then will they comprehend, understand, and take to heart, that
in folly they have cast our bodies to the ground, and for falsehood
have they slain our saints; that they have spilled the blood of
righteous women because of a putrid corpse, and over the teachings
of an agitator and misleader have they shed the blood of sucklings;
that his teachings are folly and that they do not know their Creator,
nor walk on a virtuous path or an upright way; that they were not
wise and did not take to heart Who it is that made the ocean and the
dry land; and that in all their actions they were fools and simple-
tons: good sense forsook them, and they placed their trust in folly,

neither recognizing nor declaring the Name of the living God, King of the Universe, Who is Eternal and Everlasting.

May the blood of His devoted ones stand us in good stead and be an atonement for us and for our posterity after us, and our children's children eternally, like the *'Akedah* of our Father Isaac when our Father Abraham bound him upon the altar.

These saints did not say to one another: "Have mercy on yourselves," but rather: "Let us cast our blood like water on the ground, and may it be considered before the Blessed Holy One as the blood of the gazelle and of the hart."[138] It is written in the Torah: "[Sow or ewe,] ye shall not kill it and its young both in one day";[139] but here father and son, mother and daughter, were slain in one day.

And let not the reader of this narrative think that these were the only individuals who sanctified the Name of the God of Heaven; those whom we have not specified by name or manner of death also sanctified the Holy and Revered Name. Thus have attested those few survivors who were forcibly converted. They heard with their own ears and saw with their own eyes the actions of these saints and their utterances at the time of their slaughter and murder.

May their merit, their righteousness, their piety, their wholeheartedness, and their sacrifice be a good advocate for us before the Most High; and may He deliver us from the exile of wicked Edom speedily in our day, and may our Messiah come, Amen, speedily in our day.

I will now recount how the community of Cologne conducted themselves, and how they sanctified His One and Sublime Name.

It was on the fifth of Sivan, the Eve of Pentecost, when the news came to Cologne,[140] the pleasant city, wherein was gathered the assembled flock—"And heaven brings about merit by means of meritorious individuals"[141]—Cologne, whence emanated life, sustenance, and law to our brethren so widely dispersed. The enemy began to slay them from Pentecost until the eighth of Tammuz.[142] Upon learning of the annihilation of the communities,[143] each Jew fled to a Gentile acquaintance and remained there during the two days of the festival.[144] On the morning of the third day, there was a great clamor; and the enemy arose against them and broke into the houses, looting and plundering. They destroyed the synagogue and removed the Torah Scrolls, desecrating them and casting them into the streets to be trodden underfoot. On the very day that the Torah was given, when the earth trembled and its pillars quivered,—they now tore, burned, and trod upon it—those wicked evildoers regarding whom it is said: "Robbers have entered and profaned it."[145]

Will You not punish them for these deeds? How long will You look on and remain silent while the wicked consume? "See, O Lord, and behold, how abject I am become."[146]

That very day they found a pious man, named Isaac, son of Elyakim, who had gone out of his house; the enemy seized him and brought him to their house of idolatry. He spat at them and at the object of their idolatry and he reviled and ridiculed them. And they slew him then and there in sanctification of the Name of God, because he did not desire to flee, out of respect for the festival, and also because he was happy to accept the judgment of Heaven.

They also found a distinguished woman, Mistress Rebecca. The enemy encountered her as she left her house bearing gold and silver vessels concealed in her sleeves, intending to bring them to her husband, Solomon, who had left his house and was now in the home of a Gentile friend. They took the money from her and slew her, and there the righteous woman died in sanctity.

At the same time another woman, Mistress Matrona, and the rest of the community were saved in the homes of acquaintances to which they had fled. They remained there until the bishop[147] went to his villages on the tenth day of Sivan and dispersed them amongst his seven villages,[148] in order to save them. There they remained until the New Moon of Tammuz, daily anticipating their death. They fasted daily, even on the two days of the New Moon of Tammuz, Monday and Tuesday, as well as on the following day. Thus did they fast day and night consecutively, for a period of three days.

On the third day, those in the village of Neuss were killed, for it was their [i.e., the Christians'] holiday,[149] and they had gathered there from the surrounding villages. The pious Samuel, son of Asher, was there, and he and his two sons were slain on the banks of the Rhine. They buried him in the sand near the river and hanged one of his sons at the entrance to his home to mock the Jews. There was another pious man there by the name of Isaac, the Levite. He was subjected to intense torture. Seeing him in such pain, they profaned him against his will, for he was utterly insensible as a result of their beatings. He regained consciousness and three days later returned to Cologne. He entered his house, paused there a while—just an hour— and then went to the Rhine River and drowned himself. About him and the likes of him is it said: "I will bring back from Bashan, I will bring them back from the depths of the sea."[150] He floated on the water as far as the village of Neuss, and there the water cast him ashore, near the pious man, Master Samuel, who had been slain in Neuss; and the two pious men were buried together, on the bank of the river, in one grave. They sanctified the Name of Heaven for all to behold. Gedaliah and his wife and children had been in the village of Bonn before the Crusade; they, too, were killed in the village of Neuss and truly sanctified God's Name.

That same day, the third day [of Tammuz], the enemies of the Lord came to a certain village,[151] and in the evening the Jews there also truly sanctified God's Name. Bridegrooms and beautiful brides, old men and old women, boys and girls—they all extended their necks and slaughtered one another, giving up their lives in sanctification of God's Name in the ponds around the village.[152] When the enemy approached the village, some of the pious men ascended the tower and cast themselves into the Rhine River, which flowed around the village, and perished by drowning.[153]

Only two young men were not able to die by drowning: Samuel, the bridegroom, son of Gedaliah, and Yeḥiel, son of Samuel. They were "pleasant in their lives," greatly loving each other, "and in their death they were not divided."[154] When they resolved to cast themselves into the water, they kissed each other, and held each other, and embraced each other around their shoulders, and wept to each other, saying: "Woe for our youth, for we were not given the privilege of seeing it produce offspring, and we have not attained old age. Nevertheless, let us now fall into the hand of the Lord, Who is God, Trustworthy and Merciful King. It is better for us to die here for His Great Name and walk with the righteous in the Garden of Eden than to fall into the hands of these impure uncircumcised ones and be forcibly defiled by them with their evil water."

Then came the others who had remained in the village and had not gone up on the tower; they saw those who had drowned, and found the two good friends, perfect in their righteousness, clinging closely to each other in the water. When Samuel saw that his son Yeḥiel, a handsome young man, whose appearance was like Lebanon, had cast himself into the river and had not yet perished, he shouted: "Yeḥiel, my son, my son, stretch out your neck before your father and I will offer you as a sacrifice to God. I will recite the benediction of Ritual Slaughter and you will respond, 'Amen.'" Samuel, the pious man, did as he had spoken, slaying his son with his sword in the water.

Samuel, the bridegroom, son of Gedaliah, upon hearing that his friend Yeḥiel, the righteous, had consented to be slaughtered in the water by his father, desired to emulate him. Calling to Menaḥem, the sexton of the synagogue in Cologne, he said: "By your life, take your sharp sword and inspect it carefully so that there be no flaw in it and slaughter me, too, for I cannot bear to see the death of my friend. Recite the benediction of Ritual Slaughter and I will respond, 'Amen.'"

Thus did these two pious ones act, and when they had been slaughtered together, before their souls expired, they clasped hands and died together in the river, fulfilling the Biblical verse, "And in their death they were not divided."

When Samuel the elder, the pious, father of Yeḥiel, saw this act of sanctification, he declared to Menaḥem, the pious sexton: "Menaḥem, control your emotions, like a brave man, and slaughter me with this very sword that I used to slaughter my son Yeḥiel. I have thoroughly inspected it, and it possesses no defect that would disqualify the Ritual Slaughter." So Menaḥem took the sword in his hand, inspected it carefully, and slaughtered Samuel the elder as he had slaughtered Samuel the bridegroom. Menaḥem pronounced the benediction of Ritual Slaughter, and Samuel answered "Amen." Then Menaḥem, devotee of the God of Heaven, fell upon the sword, thrusting it into his stomach, and perished there. Thus did these pious men sanctify in the water the Holy Name of the Jealous and Vengeful God.

Now, come all ye mortals, come and behold: has there been such a witness to the Oneness of God's Name since the time of Adam? How mighty is the power of these righteous men slaughtered by their own swords! How great was the fortitude of the father, who was not softened by pity for his son! Many there were who acted thus. Truly, the eye has seen and given witness, the ear has heard and attested to it.

There were also some who drowned themselves in the waters, and nothing remained but three seeds. There were also an old man, Eleazar, the Levite, father-in-law of Levi, son of Solomon, and his righteous wife, whom the enemy tortured greatly and inflicted many wounds on them in an effort to coerce them to believe in their abomination, but they refused to bear faith to the abhorrence. The righteous woman died immediately from hunger and thirst, but her pious husband lived three days, crying aloud to God-on-High to take his soul. The enemy came to him every hour, for the ponds whence they came were near the village. The enemy beat them terribly and attempted to feed them,[155] but they refused to eat. Both of them died from thirst and hunger and were buried there.

"Wilt Thou restrain Thyself for these things, O Lord?"[156] "[The Lord] will go forth as a mighty man."[157] And it is said, "Sing aloud, O ye nations, of His people; for He doth avenge the blood of His servants."[158]

There were many in those two villages[159] whom I have forgotten and they have not been recorded; they were all killed in sanctification of His Great Name. From amongst all those people, only two young men and two babes remained.

On the third of Tammuz, a Thursday, devotees of the Most High God, those of the village of Eller,[160] were slain. They, too, greatly sanctified the One Name. Not more than a few remained.

On the fourth of Tammuz, on Friday, the enemy gathered against the saints of Eller to torment them cruelly so that they would submit to be defiled. When the pious men learned of this, they confessed to their Creator. And of their own accord they chose five righteous saints, men of understanding, God-fearing men, to slaughter the others. About three hundred souls were there, the outstanding personalities of the community of Cologne, and they were all slaughtered, not a single one of them remaining, for they all died in purity in sanctification of the One Name.

Yuda, son of Abraham, the *Parnass*, leader of them all, was among them. He was a sage, a counselor, and a person of eminence.

When all the communities would come to the market in Cologne,[161] thrice yearly, he would address them in the synagogue and they would remain silent and listen attentively. And when the other communal leaders began to speak, those present shouted them down so that they could hear his words, declaring: "He speaks the truth, and his words are upright and correct." He was of the tribe of Dan,[162] a faithful man, an example for his generation. He readily went to the aid of anyone in trouble, and he never caused harm to anyone. Beloved by Heaven, popular among men, it was of him that David composed an entire Psalm, the one beginning: "A Psalm of David: Lord, who shall sojourn in Thy tabernacle?"[163]

The women also truly sanctified the Name before the eyes of all. When Sarit, the virgin bride, of beautiful form and fair to look upon and lovely in the eyes of them who beheld her, saw how they had slain themselves with their own swords and slaughtered each other, she wanted to flee from the fearful scene she witnessed from her window. When her [intended] father-in-law, Judah, son of Abraham the pious, saw what she was about to do, he called to her and said: "My daughter, since you were not fortunate to marry my son, Abraham, you will not marry anyone else—a Gentile." He took hold of her, put her out the window, and kissed her mouth, and lifted his voice together with hers in a cry, shouting bitterly to those standing there: "Behold, this is the wedding of my daughter-in-law which I will make today." And they all wept loudly, wailing, mourning, and moaning. Then the pious Judah said to her: "My daughter, come and lie in the bosom of our Father Abraham, for in a moment you will earn your eternal life and you will enter the precincts of the righteous and the pious." He took her and laid her in the bosom of his son Abraham, her fiancé, and cut her asunder with his sharp sword. He then slaughtered his son as well. From this do my eyes weep, and my heart wails.

When they had fulfilled their intention to fast three days, day and night—boy and girl, babe and suckling, along with old men—their tongues clung to their palates from thirst. Babes did not suckle at their mothers' breasts before they were slaughtered. It was on the third day that they readied themselves and made haste to perform the command of their Creator and to demonstrate their love for Him even unto death!

The pious David, son of Isaac, also afflicted himself in fasting, and he no longer had even a fourth of his blood in him; when they slaughtered him, not even a fourth of a fourth of his blood bled from him. His spirit then returned to his God and his pure soul departed. Know ye, how they sanctified the holy Name and did not have mercy on their children.

After three days, when the enemies of God had departed, those Hebrews who had been forcibly converted and to whom the enemy had shown mercy, returned to bury the dead, who had become carrion for the fowls of the heaven and the beasts of the earth. They found one women, barely alive, writhing in blood, and they washed her and brought her to a house. Seven days passed without her speaking, eating, or drinking. Afterwards, she revived, and they healed her. From that day on, she fasted constantly, eating but once a day, except on the Sabbath, the holidays, and the New Moon festival.

Up to this time, in the year [four thousand] nine hundred,[164] nine hundred, have I, Solomon bar Simson, recorded this occurrence in Mainz. There I asked the elders concerning the entire matter, and from their reports I have described each incident in its proper sequence. It was they who told me of this sanctification.

On Friday, on the fourth of the month, on Sabbath Eve at twilight, on the eve of the day of tranquility, the enemies of the Lord came to the pious people of Xanten. The enemy fell upon them just as the Sabbath was setting in and they were sitting down to eat bread, having sanctified the Sabbath by reciting "And the heavens and the earth were finished, etc.,"[165] and then said the blessing over the bread. Suddenly the voice of the oppressor was heard and the evil waters came upon them.

They had not yet begun to eat, only broken bread, and their leader said: "Son of Aaron the Priest,[166] you are worthy of greatness. Woe to those who are departed and cannot be found. Therefore is my harp turned to mourning, and my pipe into the voice of them that weep." All who heard his voice when he prayed said: "This voice is as a harp, a pipe, a drum, and a flute." His prayers went up before the throne of Him Who dwells On High, to the Presence of the Everlasting One, and became a crown and a diadem on the head

of the Most High God, the King of Kings, the Blessed Holy One. But
the decree had been passed and it was as if a copper griddle had been
placed between us and our Father in Heaven,[167] shutting out our
prayers, and we could not find even one good advocate among a
thousand. For God had come to test this generation and to demonstrate their love for Him to all, including the Host of Heaven. Thus
did King David declare: "Therefore do the maidens love thee"—
until death do they love you![168] In a similar manner he stated, "For
Thy sake are we killed all the day; we are accounted as sheep for the
slaughter."[169]

    This pious, faithful man, the priest that is highest among his
brethren, then said to the congregation assembled at his table: "Let
us recite the Grace-after-Meals to the Living God, to our Father in
Heaven, for the table is now arranged before us in place of the altar.
Let us arise and hurry to the House of the Lord to fulfill the wish of
our Creator. The enemy has come upon us today so that each man
may slaughter—on the Sabbath—his son, his daughter, and his
brothers, and so that we may thereby be blessed. Let no man have
mercy on himself or his friend. The last survivor shall slaughter himself with his knife at his throat, or shall thrust his sword into his
stomach, so that the impure ones and the hands of wickedness will
not be able to defile us with their abominations. We shall offer ourselves as a sacrifice to the Lord, as a whole-burnt-offering to the
Most High One, a sacrifice upon the altar of God. Then we shall
enter the World-that-is-All-Day, the Garden of Eden, the great
luminous speculum, and we shall behold the countenance of the
Lord in its actual Glory and Greatness. Every person will have a diadem of gold set with precious stones and pearls upon his head. We
shall sit there amongst the pillars of the world and dine in the company of the righteous in the Garden of Eden, and we shall be in the
company of Rabbi Akiba and his companions.[170] We shall sit on a
golden chair under the Tree of Life, and each of us will point with
his finger and declare: 'Lo, this is our God, for Whom we have
waited. . . . Let us be glad and rejoice in His salvation.' And there we
will observe all the Sabbaths, for here, in this world of darkness, we
are unable to rest and observe the Sabbath properly."

    They all answered loudly, with one mouth and one heart:

"Amen, so be it and so be His will." Our master, the pious Rabbi Moses, then began to say the Grace-after-Meals, for he was a priest of the Most High God,[171] and he said: "Let us bless our God of Whose bounty we have partaken," and the others responded: "Blessed be our God of Whose bounty we have partaken, and through Whose goodness we live."[172] He then declared: "May the Merciful One avenge, in the lifetime of those who will survive us and before their very eyes, Thy servants' blood that is spilt and that will yet be spilt; may the Merciful One save us from wicked men, from forced conversion, and from idolatry, from the defilement of the nations and from their abominations."[173] He also recited many other timely benedictions that referred to the impending decree. Thus did my ancestors and the other elders who were involved in the work[174] and saw this momentous happening, relate to me.

When they rose from the table, the pious man said to them: "You are the children of the Living God. Declare aloud and in unison, 'Hear, O Israel, the Lord is our God, the Lord is One,'" and they did so. "Now, do not tarry any longer, for the time has come to act—to offer up our souls to Him." On the Eve of the Sabbath, at twilight, they offered themselves as a sacrifice before God, in place of the daily evening burnt-offering, and they themselves became as the morning burnt-offering.[175]

As a man rejoices when he finds booty, and as [one feels] the joy of the harvest, so were they joyful and elated to perform the service of our God and to sanctify His Great and Holy Name. And they all came, happily and joyfully, before the High and Mighty God. Concerning the likes of them it is stated: "[He is] as a bridegroom coming out of his chamber; and rejoiceth as a strong man to run his course."[176] So did they rejoice to run and to enter into the innermost chambers of the Garden of Eden. It is of them that the Prophet declared: "Neither hath the eye seen a God beside Thee, Who worketh for him that waiteth for Him."[177]

Natronai, son of Isaac, a wholehearted man, was also there. His acquaintances the priests had come to him throughout the entire previous day attempting to persuade him to defile himself in their evil waters, for he was a handsome man, pleasant to the sight. He threw a branch in their faces[178] and said: "God forbid that I should deny God-on-High; I will trust in Him until my soul expires." He slaughtered his brother and then himself, in witness to the Oneness of the One Holy Name.

There was also a servant of God there, a sincere proselyte, who inquired of Rabbi Moses. the great priest: "Master, if I slaughter myself in witness to the Oneness of His Great Name, what will become of me?" He replied: "You will abide with us in our company; for you will be a true proselyte, and you will dwell in the company of the other true proselytes—you will be with our Father Abraham who was the first proselyte." When the pious man heard this, he immediately took the knife and slaughtered himself; and behold, his soul is bound up in the bond of those who live in the Garden of Eden in God's light.

In this *Akedah* not one survived except for those who were lacerated and wallowed in the blood amongst the dead. When the enemy had captured the tower—before they could get around to slaying everyone—they fled in the night from fear of the dead, and all the dead received burial, praised be the Creator. May their merit and the merit of the others who were slaughtered, stabbed, strangled, burned, drowned stoned. and buried alive—accepting upon themselves, with love and affection, seven deaths, corresponding to the days of the week, in witness to the Holy and Pure Fear—be good advocates for us before the Most High God, so that He may redeem us speedily from the exile of wicked Edom, speedily in our day, and rebuild for us the walls of *Ariel*,[179] and gather in the scattered ones of Judah and Israel who are dispersed, as with a winnowing fork, to all the portals of the earth—the remnant that took refuge and remained to suffer imprisonment, pillage, adversity, and distress among the Gentiles. May He do so for the sake of His Great, Mighty, and Awesome Name by which we are called.

On a Sunday, in the month of Tammuz,[180] the enemies of God also rose against the saints of the Most High of the town of Mehr to annihilate them. There besieged the city a multitude as numerous as the grains of sand upon the seashore. The mayor of the city went out to meet them in the field and asked them to wait until daybreak. He spoke thus: "Perhaps I can coax the Jews and they, out of fear, will heed me and do as I ask." This found favor in their eyes, and the mayor immediately returned to the Jews in the city. He had them summoned and brought before him, and he said to them: "In truth I originally vowed to you that I would shelter and protect you as long as there was yet a single Jew alive. I have fulfilled this pledge to you. Henceforth, however, I am unable to protect you from all these nations. Decide now what you wish to do. Know that if you do not do thus-and-so, the city will be completely destroyed. I would rather hand you over to them than have them besiege the city and destroy the fortress."

Young and old, they all replied in unison: "We are ready and eager to extend our throats attesting to the fear of our Creator and the Oneness of His Name." When the mayor saw that he was unable to sway them, he immediately tried another ploy—in an effort to frighten them—and led them to the outskirts of the city to the site where the errant ones were encamped, hoping that they would thus be intimidated into submitting to defilement. But it was all to no avail, for they all said: "We are not afraid of the errant ones."

When they [the mayor and the burghers] saw that their ploy was to no effect, they returned them to the city and imprisoned them, each one separately, until the morrow, so that they would not slay each other, as they heard that the others had done. The next day they handed them over to the errant ones. who, as they were hurriedly being driven from the city, killed some of them; those whom they allowed to live they forcibly defiled and did with them as they wished.

A pious man named Shemariah escaped together with his wife and three sons on that night; the bishop's bursar had promised to take him along and save him in return for a large sum of money which he had given him. The bursar led them this way and that in the forest until the ninth of Av,[181] and then sent to Shemariah's sons in Speyer, Nathan and Mordecai, for money. They dispatched *zehuvim*.[182] Upon getting the money, he immediately took them and handed them over to the village of Tremonia.[183] When Shemariah arrived there, the villagers rejoiced, for they recognized him. The townspeople agreed to the request of the Jews to wait until the next day and then to do as they desired.

They immediately made a merry feast. The Jews would not join them in their disgusting repast, but would only eat in purity, and only that which is ritually permissible, using a new knife, for they said: "While we yet adhere to our faith, we desire to act in accordance with our custom; tomorrow we will all be one people. Place us in one room overnight, until tomorrow, for we are weary and tired from the road." So the townspeople did as the pious man had told them, granting him his request. He [Shemariah] rose in the night, took the knife in his hand, mustered up his strength, and slaughtered his wife and three sons. He tried to slaughter himself, too, but fainted and did not die.

The following day, when the enemy came, they thought that they [Shemariah and his family] would come over to them as he had promised; instead, they found him lying on the ground. They asked him: "Do you want to change your God, and to adopt our erroneous belief,[184] so that you may yet live?" He replied: "God forbid! I will not deny a living God for one that is dead, a rotting corpse; I would rather be killed for the sake of the Name of the Blessed Holy One and His Holy Torah, and today I will come into the company of the righteous. All my life I hoped for this day."

They said: "We will not kill you, as you think. We will bury you alive in the tomb unless you accept our erroneous belief." He repeated: "Let it be as you say, for I accept everything upon me with love." The evil men dug him a pit, and Shemariah, the pious man, entered on his own power. He took his three sons and laid them at his left, and his wife at his right, and he lay down in the middle. They threw earth upon him from above, and all that day until the following morning he shrieked and wept aloud and keened for himself and his sons and his wife lying next to him.

The enemies of the Lord returned and removed him from the grave while he was still alive, so that he might recant and acknowledge their erroneous faith. Again they asked him: "Do you want to change your God?" But the pious Shemariah did not wish to exchange the Great and the Venerable for the ignoble, and he remained firm in his integrity till his soul departed. They placed him in the grave again and cast earth upon him; and there the pious man died in witness to the Oneness of the Venerable and Awesome Name. He withstood his trial as our Father Abraham did—happy is he and happy is his lot.

It is of him and the likes of him that it is written: "They that love Him are as the sun when it goeth forth in its might."[185] When is the sun "in its might"? In the season of Tammuz.[186] Now work it out: Just as the sun is more intense in the season of Tammuz than it is all the other days of the year, in the World-to-Come the righteous will be above all nations. And they will be in that group which is dearer to God than all others, and they are destined to stand and abide in the shade of the Blessed Holy One and to stand at His right hand, as it is written: "At His right hand was a fiery law unto them."[187] It is of them that Scripture states: "In Thy presence is fulness of joy, in Thy right hand bliss forevermore."[188] Do not read "fulness" but rather "seven,"[189] and this refers to the seven groups of the righteous, each higher than the next, their faces resembling the sun and the moon. Regarding them, it is said, "Oh, how abundant is Thy goodness, which Thou hast laid up for them that fear Thee; which Thou has wrought for them that take their refuge in Thee." "They shall ever shout for joy." "Light is sown for the righteous, and joy for the upright in heart."[190] These righteous men desired to santify the Venerable and Awesome Name with joyfulness and with gladness of heart like one who goes to a house of feasting, and they longed to attest His Oneness as the hart panteth after the brooks of water.

Of all those seven villages to which the community of Cologne had dispersed, no one was saved except for the few in the village of Kerpen, who were not slain. But the hostile mayor of the village perpetrated evil in another manner; for, by his command, his servants took the gravestones of the dead buried in Cologne to build him an edifice out of these gravestones.[191] And that is what they did. When, however, they raised the stones on the ramparts of the building to build a wall, it happened—by the intervention of the jealous and vengeful God—that a stone fell on the head of the enemy, the mayor of the village, cracking his skull and shattering his brain, and he died. Afterwards his wife went out of her mind and lost control of her senses and died from that illness. Thus did the jealous and vengeful God give us a sign that He had wrought vengeance upon them for what they had done.

So may He speedily in our days avenge the blood of His servants that is being spilt daily for His sake.

The enemies carried out their evil intentions in these communities, as we have related, and in other communities as well: in Trier, in Metz, in Regensburg, in Prague,[192] in Wesseli and in Bohemia.[193] The Jews all sanctified the Great and Awesome Name with love and devotion. All of this happened in that year at the same time,[194] for the Lord had chosen that entire good generation for His portion, to provide merit, by virtue of their actions for the generations to come. And may it indeed be the will of the High and Exalted God to grant their descendants after them the reward for the deeds of their ancestors, and may their merit. their righteousness, their piety, and their virtue stand us in good stead eternally, Selah, to hasten the Final Redemption and to guide us eternally in the land of the living.

The entire account of Trier[195] has been related to me. On the fifteenth day of Nisan, the first day of Passover, a messenger came from France to the errant ones—a "messenger of Jesus" by the name of Petron. He was a priest and was called Peter Prälat.[196] When he arrived in Trier, accompanied by many men, on his crooked path to Jerusalem, he bore with him a letter from the Jews of France, saying that wherever the sole of his foot should tread passing through Jewish areas, he should be given provision for the journey and he would speak kindly of Israel—for he was a priest and his words would be heeded.[197] When he came here, our souls went out, our hearts broke, trembling took hold of us and our feast was turned into mourning; for until now the burghers had not spoken of doing any evil to the community—before the arrival of those depraved ones.

They [the Jews of Trier] gave to the priest Peter and he continued on his way. Then our evil neighbors. the burghers, came, jealous concerning what had happened in the other communities of Lorraine:[198] they had heard that great misfortunes had been inflicted and decreed upon the Jews. They [the Jews] now took their money and bribed the burghers but all this was to no avail on the day of the Lord's fierce anger, for it was a dispensation brought about by God, from Heaven, on that entire generation which had been chosen for His portion, to fulfill His commandment.

At that time the people of the community of Trier took their Torah Scrolls and placed them in a sturdy building. When the enemies became aware of this. they went there while it was still day and broke the roof above; they took all the mantles and the silver adorning the rollers of the Torah, and threw the Torah Scrolls on the ground, and tore them and trod upon them with their feet The Jews had already fled to the bishop,[199] but he was not there. So, taking along some of the officers and servants of the bishop they knowingly endangered their lives and returned to the house where they found the Torah Scrolls trodden underfoot. They rent their clothing and cried out bitterly: "Behold. O Lord. my affliction. for the enemy hath magnified himself."[200]

They took the Torah Scrolls lifting them from the ground. kissed them, and hastened with them to the protective custody of the palace. During that time they fasted much. repented, and gave charity. They fasted six weeks. not partaking of any food during the day,[201] from Passover to 'Azeret.[202] Every morning they would generously distribute charity among the poor. They imposed a tax; on four occasions they gave a *dinar* out of every pound. But it was still inadequate to cover the many bribes. and they continued thus until they had exhausted all their possessions. even the cloaks on their shoulders. They finally decided to give everything they possessed to the bishop, so that he would save them from the evil doers. This was of no avail whatever, for God had given them over to their enemies and had kindled His wrath upon them and had concealed His face from them on their day of reckoning.[203]

The first day of Pentecost was a market day. A religious procession was to take place, and Crusaders came by way of the Rhine River to the market. The pious Jews, men of holiness, fled to the Palais, the palace of the bishop. The murderers came boasting of the killing and destruction that they had inflicted upon famed men of holy communities.

The bishop came to the church of St. Simon[204] so as to protect the Jews. When the enemies heard the sermon of the bishop, in which he mentioned the Jews, they assembled in order to attack him. The bishop fled inside the church, concealing himself in one of the rooms, where he remained for a week. All the Gentiles came to the Palais, in which the children of the Sacred Covenant had taken refuge, in order to war against them. but they were unable to do so. The enemy's heart wavered as the movement of trees in the forest before a wind when they saw the obstructing wall; for it was very strong, five cubits in width, and as high as the eye could see; and the enemy withdrew. They then thought to kill the bishop in the church of St. Simon; the bishop was very much frightened because he was a stranger in the city and had neither relative nor acquaintance there, and thus had no power to save the Jews. The bishop then went to the Jews, offering them counsel: "What do you desire to do? You see for yourselves that Jews have been slain in all your surroundings. It was my desire to fulfill my pledge to you till the very end, till the last community remained in the kingdom of Lorraine. Now you see for yourselves that the errant ones have risen against me to slay me. I still fear them, and I have been fleeing from them for the past fifteen days."

The community replied: "Did you not guarantee to protect us till the king returned?"[205] He answered: "The king himself cannot save you from the marked ones [i.e., the Crusaders]. Convert, or accept upon yourselves the judgment of Heaven." They responded: "Know that if each of us had ten souls, we would give them up in witness to the Oneness of His Name, rather than let them defile us." They then stretched out their necks and said: "We will give up our heads rather than deny our God!" When the bishop saw this, he left with his officers and arranged for a four-day delay, until after the Day of the Giving of the Torah, for thus had the pious men requested. They made that holiday a day of mourning, for they now realized, and had been informed, that the bishop and all who open their mouths wide[206] were plotting evil against them for no cause.

That day, the bishop sent a messenger to them asking for counsel, for the entire horde had risen against him to slay him. They thought that he wanted them to bribe him, so they told the messenger to offer him all their money. The messenger, however, answered by saying: "The bishop does not desire this." The hands of the pious men thereupon grew feeble. The hearts of the bishop and his officers then changed toward them for evil. They took counsel together and decided not to slay all of the Jews, but to kill two or three of them, in order to cause the hearts of the remaining to grow faint, and perhaps thus coerce them to accept the erroneous belief.

The bishop summoned the notables of the city and his officers, and they stood before the palace gate. In the gateway was a door, like the mouth of a furnace, and the enemy stood surrounding the Palais, in the hundreds and thousands, holding sharpened swords and ready to consume them [the Jews] alive, body and flesh. The commander and the officers of the bishop's palace guard then entered the Palais and declared: "Thus did our lord the bishop say: convert or leave his palace. He no longer wishes to protect you, for several times many have risen against him to slay him because of you; but you cannot be saved, for your God does not wish to deliver you now as He did in olden times."

They saw the great multitude standing before the palace gate. When they saw that, the grief was very great, the pious ones came, sat on the ground, raised their voices in a cry, and wept sorely with bitterness of heart—men, women, and children—and they confessed their sins. They then led Asher, son of Joseph, the *Gabbai*, outside to kill him, so as to instill fear and terror in the rest so that they would acknowledge their error. Asher called out: "Who amongst you of the entire nation of the Lord—may his God be with him—will come forward: one who desires to receive and welcome the Divine Presence—and in that world which lavishes an abundance of goodness in the space of a few moments?" A youth named Meir, the son of Samuel, spoke up and said: "Wait, I desire to accompany you to the World-that-is-All-Light, and with you I will bear witness to the Oneness of the One, Venerable, and Awesome Name—wholeheartedly and willingly." When they emerged from the door of the Palais, the crucified one was brought before them so that they would bow to him. They cast a branch at the abomination,[207] and the two pious men were slain in sanctification of the Name.

Abraham, son of Yom Tov, was present; he was a faithful man, righteous, upright, and beloved of God. It was his custom to attend the synagogue both in the morning and in the evening. Master Abraham fell forward upon his face and confessed his iniquities before the blessed King of Kings. He lifted up his voice and cried: "I beseech You, O Lord, God! Why have you abandoned your nation, Israel, to derision, contempt, and humiliation, to be consumed by nations impure as swine—this very people whom You chose to be the elect of all the nations, whom You raised up from earth to the firmament? And now that splendrous Israel Thou hast cast down from heaven to earth, and many are the slain that You have caused amongst us!" The pious man prostrated himself completely on the earth before everyone. The enemy lifted him up, led him outside, and there he was slain in sanctification of the Name. A little girl was present, daughter of a distinguished family, and she also sanctified the Name in holiness.

After these had been slain, the enemy saw that those remaining within the Palais were still as firm in their faith as they had been originally, nor had their hands turned feeble as a result of what had happened to the others. The enemies said to one another: "All this is because the wives are inciting their husbands to remain firm in their defiance of the crucified one." The officers came, and each one seized the hands of the women, striking and inflicting wounds upon them, and led them to the idolatry in order to defile them. Then they ordered children snatched from their mothers' boscms, thereby fulfilling what is written: "Thy sons and thy daughters shall be given unto another people."[208] And the women lifted up their voices and wept.

Three days before these acts of coercion, the officers had come into the Palais and blocked up the well inside, lest the Jewesses slay their children by casting them into the well. Nor did they allow them to mount the wall, lest they throw themselves off it. They guarded them the entire night so that they would not kill each other before dawn. All this they devised because they did not wish to kill them, but to capture and forcibly convert them.

A girl standing by the door of the Palais extended her neck outside and said: "Anyone who desires to sever my head—so that I may thus attest the faith of my God—let him come and do so." However, the uncircumcised ones did not wish to harm her, for this maiden was of beautiful form and possessed of grace. But they repeatedly tried to take her with them forcibly—they tried but did not succeed, for she would throw herself to the ground feigning death. Thus she remained in the Palais. Her aunt approached her and said, "Do you wish to die with me faithful to our Rock?" She replied: "Yes, gladly!" They bribed the guard at the gate, went onto the bridge, and cast themselves into the water in witness to the King of the Universe. Two maidens from Cologne did the same. It is of them and the likes of them that it is written: "Thus said the Lord: 'I will bring back from Bashan, I will bring them back from the depths of the sea.'"[209] Praise the Lord that they were later brought to burial. May the Avenger in our days and before our eyes avenge the spilt blood of His servants, and may their merit and righteousness stand us in good stead and protect us on the day of evil.

I will now relate what befell the people of Metz.[210] O Lord, you have utterly rejected Israel. You soul abhorred the holy community of Metz; why were they and their children smitten? Why were the holy devotees of the Most High, the honorable of the earth,[211] masters of Torah, slain there? Samuel Cohen, the *Gabbai*, and many others were slaughtered there, all titans and saints, the very foundations of the earth. Twenty-two people were slain there,[212] and the majority were forcibly converted—because of our many sins and great guilt. The forced converts remained there until the day of indignation passed,[213] and afterwards they returned to the Lord with all their heart; may God accept their penitence and forgive the sins of His people.

The entire community in Regensburg[214] was forcibly converted, for they saw that they could not be saved. When the errant ones and the rest of the mob gathered, the people of the city forced them into the river [i.e., to baptize them], and then the enemy made an evil sign over the water—vertical and horizontal [i.e., a cross] —and defiled them all simultaneously in that river, for there was a great multitude there. They, too, returned to the Lord as soon as the enemy had left, doing great penance.[215] For what they had done, they had done under powerful duress, being unable to withstand the enemy, and the enemy had not wished to slay them. May God forgive us our trespasses.

The errant ones came to the prominent men, men of sanctity, who were in the city of Šla,[216] and said: "Now give heed carefully to our words and you will know in what manner to act. Accept our mistaken belief [i.e., adopt our faith], or submit to a judgment of death, as did your brethren who dwell in the land of Hori."[217] They requested three days from the errant ones and their townsmen. Word of this plea was in turn conveyed by a messenger to the overlord. Those three days were sanctified with a fast, and they entreated the Living God with fasting, tears, and outcry. Their prayers were accepted and the Merciful God saved them. During the three days of

respite their overlord came to their aid and sent a duke with one
thousand mounted swordsmen; also amongst the Jews dwelling in the
city of Šla were five hundred young men who could bear swords, men
of war who would not waver in the face of the enemy. The army
confidently came upon the city and greatly smote the errant ones
and townsmen. Of the Jews, only six were killed. The Luminary of
Israel rescued the others and led them all together to a certain town
facing the city which was not on the bank of the river. There they
remained in peace and quiet until the enemies of the Lord departed.

It is now fitting to recount the praises of those who were
forcibly converted. They risked their lives even in matters pertaining
to food and drink. They slaughtered the animals they ate in accordance with Jewish ritual, extracted the forbidden fat, and inspected
the meat in accordance with Rabbinic law. They did not drink pro-
hibited wine and rarely attended church, and whenever they did go,
it was under great coercion and fear, and they went with aggrieved
spirits. The Gentiles themselves knew that they had not converted
out of conviction but rather in fear of the errant ones, and that the
Jews did not believe in the object of their reverence but remained
steadfast in their reverence for the Lord and clung firmly to the
Most High God, Creator of heaven and earth. In the eyes of the
Gentiles they observed the Gentile Sabbath properly; but they
observed God's Torah clandestinely. He who speaks evil of them, it
is as though he spoke thus of the Divine Countenance.

And it came to pass after these occurrences, after they had fulfilled their will and desire, that they [i.e., the Crusaders] continued
on their misguided path to Jerusalem. The first contingent was under
the leadership of a priest from France,[218] accompanied by a large
army. Arriving at the border of the kingdom of Hungary, he sent
messengers to the king of Hungary,[219] declaring: "Let us pass
through your land; we will go by the king's highway and will neither
eat nor drink without money."[220] The king granted the Crusaders
permission to pass through his entire land, but they were to proceed
in a peaceful manner and not harm his subjects in any city.

They came to a large fortified city, with was heavily populated.
Wounded by arrows of famine, the army paid a *dinar*[221] for a small
amount of bread. One of the errant ones carried woolen garters to

sell in the marketplace so that he could buy bread. A townsman came and ridiculed him, and Satan intervened, and they fought murderously with each other. An evil spirit came between the Crusaders and the townsmen, and the misled ones rose up and slew the entire city, down to infant and suckling. The king heard what had occurred.

The enemies of the Lord departed from there and arrived at the River Danube; the river was overflowing its banks and no boats were available. Near the river was a small village. The Crusaders came and destroyed the village, and took the wood of the houses to use as logs, from which they built a bridge and crossed the river. They arrived at the bolted gates of the walled city,[222] the inhabitants of the city having shut the gates so as to prevent them from entering. The king, aware of their advance, had commanded that the Crusaders be denied entry to the fortified city lest they destroy his kingdom, and the people complied with his decree.

Peter the Priest, seeing that he would be unable to enter, sent a priest as emissary to the city, saying: "Since you forbid us to enter the city, send out bread to us and we will buy it." The people refused, in conformity with the king's command. He persisted and sent messengers to the city guard, asking that they sell them bread worth one *ma'ah* for two.[223] They replied: "Even if your lives depend on it, we will not sell to you."

That night the enemies of the Lord fasted and they all came to Peter the Priest to seek counsel. They said: "Tomorrow let us take revenge upon them." Peter replied, "Indeed this is a worthless and faithless nation, of even less trustworthiness than the Ishmaelites. They actually deserve to be stoned to death,[224] for by their own testimony they are wholly unconcerned about whether we live or not." He then called to his people and said: "Surround the city!" The Crusaders attacked the city, smashed the gates, and slew all those within. They remained in the city for three days, eating all that they could find, then plundered the city, and departed.

The king of Hungary learned what the Crusaders had done—how they had destroyed two of his cities—and his heart melted. He assembled his entire army to do battle against the errant ones, for they were very great in number, an assemblage as multitudinous as the grains of sand upon the seashore. He then commanded his officers to tell the people to return to their homes, but to be in constant preparedness to return to the king upon his command.

The next day the king summoned only the officers, knights, and deputies. They took counsel with the king and decided to shut the gates on the borders of the kingdom of Hungary, so that henceforth not a single errant one might enter. As to those who had already entered—they began to slay those who lagged behind. Upon capturing a group of a hundred errant ones, they would slay them; they repeated this procedure on the next day and the day after that, until they had slain all those accompanying Peter the Priest. And the Blessed Holy One avenged upon them the blood of His servants, and not a single man of them remained alive.[225]

The kingdom of Hungary was strongly fortified because of the enemy. Then came the army of the Rhine, composed of the inhabitants of the Rhine—a very great army; also the Swabian army and the army of France, as well as the Austrian army, who are the sons of Seir who dwell in Hori—an immense horde as numerous as the grains of sand upon the seashore. At their head was the evil Emicho, count of Leiningen, may his bones be ground to dust! They arrived at the Hungarian border, at the city of Wieselburg.[226] Clay pits surrounded the city. They tried to attack the city but were unsuccessful. The leaders and the counts decided to send emissaries to the king of Hungary, requesting that for the sake of the crucified one he grant them passage, assuring him that they would not wield their arms. The counts chose four of their number to bear this message. The king ordered them imprisoned for four days; on the third day, the four noblemen swore to the king that they would bring him the head of Count Emicho, and he then released them unharmed.

Emicho was informed of the matter, and he fled in the night; and the remnant also fled. The army of the king of Hungary pursued them and inflicted a great toll on them, more perishing and drowning in the deep marshes than were slain by the sword. A person fleeing would sink into the swamp up to his knees, and, unable to move from there, would finally perish. The Greeks[227] pursued them from all sides till the Danube River. They fled across the bridge which Peter the Priest had made, and it broke. More than thousands—tens of thousands[228]—drowned in the Danube River, until they walked on the backs of the drowned as if on dry land. The survivors came and told us, and our hearts rejoiced, for the Lord had shown us vengeance against our enemies.[229]

At that time there was an eclipse of the sun;[230] on that day the Lord shattered the pride of our enemies, and their name was uprooted. But the enemies still did not give up their evil designs, and daily they set out for Jerusalem. The Lord gave them over as sheep to be slaughtered and sanctified them for the day of slaying. "Render unto our neighbors sevenfold into their bosom." "Thou wilt render unto them a recompense, O Lord, according to the work of their hands. Thou wilt give them hardness of heart; Thy curse unto them. Thou wilt pursue them in anger, and destroy them from under the heavens of the Lord."[231] "For the Lord hath a day of vengeance, a year of recompense for the controversy of Zion."[232] "O Israel that are saved by the Lord with an everlasting salvation; ye shall not be ashamed nor confounded, forever."[233]

When we first came to Speyer,[234] it was with the hope that we pitch our tent forever, never having to uproot its stakes. We settled there because of the conflagration in Mainz—the city of Mainz, our birthplace, the place of our fathers, that ancient community, famed and praised beyond all the communities of the realm. The entire Jewish section and their street [that of the Gentiles] in Mainz were burned, and we were in great fear of the townspeople.[235] At that time, Meir Cohen arrived from Worms bearing a Torah. Persons thinking that it was gold or silver slew him. According to the order of Creation, it was the year of: "Shall the priest and the prophet be slain in the sanctuary of the Lord?"[236] Our master, Rabbi Meshullam,[237] said to them [the Jews]: "Now you need not fear, for his death overweighs and atones for our transgression."[238]

We then decided to leave and seek settlement in a fortified city. Perhaps the Gracious Lord would be gracious unto us and the Merciful One would have mercy and He-Who-Aids would help to preserve us alive, as at this day. He [the bishop][239] received us kindly and dispatched his officers and horsemen to accompany us. He then gave us quarters in the city and said that he would build around us a wall with a bolted gate so as to protect us from oppressors; it would thus be a fortress for us. He was compassionate to us, like a father to his son.

We offered prayer to our Creator, morning and evening daily, and we were saved by the Bishop John. Eleven were killed, but the rest of the community was saved, may his memory be blessed and raised.[240]

We then returned to the city, each man to his home and to his place. But those of the upper quarter could not go to the lower quarter of the city in the evening, morning, or afternoon, for fear of the cursed oppressors;[241] so we prayed in the upper quarter, in the *beth midrash*[242] of our Master Rabbi Judah, son of Rabbi Kalonymos, while those in the lower quarter prayed in their house of worship. This custom remained for some years.

The entire labor was completed in the month of Elul,[243] in the year 4864.[244] On the eve of *Rosh ha-Shanah*[245] one of the elders came and declared to the community: "Come, let us go up to the land, to the house which we have established on its foundation and built completely." The elders of the community, the priests, and the Levites went, taking the Torah Scrolls to the ark in the synagogue with great joy, and the Scrolls have remained there to the present day. On the following day, *Rosh ha-Shanah*, we began to pray in it, and we have prayed there to this day.

This is the end.

May God grant that we see the rebuilding of the Temple speedily in our days, and that we behold the graciousness of the Lord and visit His Temple, and may He comfort us in our mourning, Amen.

The Chronicle of
Rabbi Eliezer
bar Nathan

INTRODUCTION

The Chronicle of Rabbi Eliezer bar Nathan is unique among the
Hebrew chronicles of the First Crusade in that substantial biographi-
cal information exists concerning the author. Bar Nathan was born
about 1090 and apparently lived until 1170. As a young man he
studied under several prominent Talmudic scholars of the time, including Rabbi Isaac bar Asher, first and foremost of the Tosaphists—
French and German Jewish writers of critical and explanatory
addenda to the Talmud during the twelfth to fourteenth centuries.
His grandson, Rabbi Eliezer bar Joel ha-Levi (Rabiah), was one of
the great German Talmudists of the twelfth century.

In later Tosaphist literature, Rabbi Eliezer bar Nathan is also
referred to as Rabbi Eliezer the Elder, or Rabbi Eliezer of Mainz,
the town where he lived, though he evidently spent some time in
Cologne. Not only was Bar Nathan a man of many skills, he was also
a remarkable traveler for his time. Apparently, he visited France,
and, in travels through the Slavic countries (referred to as "the land
of Canaan" in his responsa), he may have gone as far as Kiev. His
legal opinions, found in the compilation entitled *'Even Ha-'Ezer*
(*Ṣofnat Pa'aneaḥ*), in fact mention customs of the distant lands to
the east, some undoubtedly reaching him through the tales of
travelers.

In addition to his scholarly activities, Bar Nathan devoted much
of his time to liturgical poetry. More than twenty-five of his poems

survive, including supplementary prayers (*yoṣrot*) for various com-
memorative sabbaths, liturgical poems for special evening services,
and several lamentations based upon the First and Second Crusades.
Several of his works entered the standard liturgies of the German
and Polish Jewish communities.

In addition to these works, Bar Nathan wrote the following
chronicle, *Gezerot TaTNU* (The Persecutions of 1096). Describing
the destruction of the Rhenish communities during the First Crusade, the chronicle also includes four short lamentations, each dedi-
cated to a specific community. The first mourns the attacks of the
Crusaders on Speyer, the second mourns the Jews of Worms, the
third those of Mainz, and the last, and longest, the attacks on the
Jews of Cologne.

Bar Nathan's chronicle is considerably shorter and, aside from
the events at Cologne, less complete than that of Bar Simson.
Indeed, apart from the liturgical segments, his chronicle can be seen
as borrowed from the same parent sources utilized by Bar Simson, or
possibly even from earlier versions of Bar Simson's own account.

The prose of Bar Nathan's chronicle is highly emotional, the
tone more prophetic and more apocalyptic than the detailed narrative style of Bar Simson or the stark realism of the anonymous
chronicler of *The Narrative of the Old Persecutions.*

Having derived from the same parent sources, the Bar Simson
chronicle and the Bar Nathan chronicle seldom contradict each
other. Most discrepancies can be attributed to the reporting of
several place-names neglected by Bar Simson, and the omission of
others mentioned by him. As for statistics, the major disparity con-
cerns the death toll at Mainz. While Bar Simson reports eleven
hundred slain, Bar Nathan raises the number of the martyred to
thirteen hundred. In contrast, certain Christian sources lowered the
number to nine hundred, and even to as low as seven hundred.[1]

Because of Bar Nathan's fame as a Talmudic scholar and a
liturgist, his chronicle enjoyed a greater degree of popularity than
did either of the two other chronicles of the First Crusade. That Bar
Nathan's account was indeed more widespread is evident from the
greater number of manuscripts extant. The following translation
utilized the oldest of the known manuscripts (No. 2797, fol. 232, of
Neubauer's *Catalogue of the Hebrew Manuscripts in the Bodleian*

Library),[2] dating no later than 1325. The three other known manuscripts ranging from the seventeenth to the nineteenth century, are identical with the earlier manuscript employed here.[3]

The popularity of Bar Nathan's account is evidenced by its subsequent adaptations by various writers of the later Middle Ages. Joseph ha-Cohen, in his *'Emek ha-Bakha (Vale of Tears)* (c. 1575), utilized Bar Nathan's chronicle in his own account of the First Crusade. A Yiddish-German translation of this chronicle can be found in the *Ma'aseh Nissim* (Miraculous Deeds) of Jospe, *Shammash* of Worms (c. 1650), printed in Amsterdam in 1696. I. Sonne mentions fragments of a Yiddish translation of an account of the First Crusade, written during the sixteenth century in Germany, perhaps constituting an even earlier Yiddish adaptation of Bar Nathan's account.[4]

The Hebrew *Chronicle of Rabbi Eliezer bar Nathan* was first published by A. Jelinek in Leipzig, 1854, under the title *Zur Geschichte der Kreuzzüge nach handschriftlichen hebräischen Quellen.*

The opening pages of a manuscript of *The Chronicle of Rabbi Eliezer bar Nathan*, from the fourteenth century. In the first of these

The Chronicle of Rabbi Eliezer bar Nathan

In the year four thousand eight hundred and fifty-six, according to the chronology of the creation of the world: the year one thousand twenty-eight of our exile, in the eleventh year of the cycle *Ranu*, the year in which we anticipated salvation and solace, in accordance with the prophecy of Jeremiah: "Sing with gladness for Jacob [and rejoice at the head of the nations]"—this year turned instead to sorrow and groaning, weeping and outcry. Much hardship and adversity befell us, the like of which had not occurred in this kingdom from the time it was established till the present. All the misfortunes related in all the admonitions written in the twenty-four books, those enumerated in Scripture as well as those unwritten, befell us and our souls. Our sons and our daughters, our elders and our youth, our servants and our maidservants, our young and old alike were all stricken by this great vicissitude.

There arose arrogant people, a people of strange speech, a nation bitter and impetuous, Frenchmen and Germans, from all directions. They decided to set out for the Holy City, there to seek their house of idolatry, banish the Ishmaelites, and conquer the land for themselves. They decorated themselves prominently with their signs, by marking themselves upon their garments with their sign—a horizontal line over a vertical one—every man and woman whose heart yearned to go there, until their ranks swelled so that the number of men, women, and children exceeded a locust horde; of them it was said: "The locusts have no king [yet go they forth all of them by bands]."

Now it came to pass that as they passed through the towns where Jews dwelled, they said to themselves: "Look now, we are going to seek out our profanity and to take vengeance on the Ishmaelites for our messiah, when here are the Jews who murdered and crucified him. Let us first avenge ourselves on them and exterminate them from among the nations so that the name of Israel will no longer be remembered, or let them adopt our faith and acknowledge the offspring of promiscuity.

When the Jewish communities learned of this, they were overcome by fear, trembling, and pains, as of a woman in travail. They resorted to the custom of their ancestors: prayer, charity, and repentance. They decreed fast days, scattered days as well as consecutive ones, fasting for three consecutive days, night and day. They cried to the Lord in their trouble, but He obstructed their prayer, concealing Himself in a cloud through which their prayers could not pass. For it had been decreed by Him to take place "in the day when I visit,"[1] and this was the generation that had been chosen by Him to be His portion, for they had the strength and the fortitude to stand in His Sanctuary, and fulfill His word, and sanctify His Great Name in His world. It is of such as these that King David said: "Bless the Lord, ye angels of His, ye mighty in strength, that fulfill His word."[2]

That year, Passover fell on Thursday, and the New Moon of the following month, Iyar, fell on Friday and the Sabbath. On the eighth day of Iyar, on the Sabbath, the foe attacked the community of Speyer and murdered ten holy souls who sanctified their Creator on the holy Sabbath and refused to defile themselves by adopting the faith of their foe. There was a pious woman there who slaughtered herself in sanctification of God's Name. She was the first among all the communities of those who were slaughtered. The remainder were saved by the local bishop without defilement.

It is about these pious ones that I will now lift my voice in lamentation:

Lament, O surpassing community, that bore witness to the Oneness
    of its Rock, like the ten who were martyred.[3]
You appointed her Your sentinel
    and with one heart and one consent she extended her neck.

You are most lovely among the celestial and lower beings, O band of
Speyer; beauteous[4] is your heritage,
Community of exultation, ever-pleasing, destined for expiation,
guardian of the vineyards.[5]
The holy couple,[6] in the month of Ziv,[7] is vested in its glory, to
be cited in the Book of Life.
Recorded and sealed, a treasured crown, by the King's decree.

As it is said: ". . . occupied in the work of the King."[8]

On the twenty-third day of Iyar the steppe-wolves attacked the
community of Worms. Some of the community were at home, and
some in the court of the local bishop. The enemies and oppressors
set upon the Jews who were in their homes, pillaging, and murdering
men, women, and children, young and old. They destroyed the
houses and pulled down the stairways, looting and plundering; and
they took the holy Torah, trampled it in the mud of the streets, and
tore it and desecrated it amidst ridicule and laughter. They devoured
Israel with open maw, saying: "Certainly this is the day that we
hoped for; we have found, we have seen it."[9]

They left only a few alive and had their way with them, forcibly
immersing them in their filthy waters; and the later acts of those
thus coerced are testimony to this beginning, for in the end they
regarded the object of the enemy's veneration as no more than slime
and dung. Those who were slain sanctified the Name for all the
world to see, and exposed their throats for their heads to be severed
for the glory of the Creator, also slaughtering one another—man, his
friend, his kin, his wife, his children, even his sons-in-law and
daughters-in-law; and compassionate women slaying their only
children—all wholeheartedly accepting the judgment of Heaven upon
themselves, and as they yielded up their souls to the Creator, they all
cried out: "Hear, O Israel, the Lord is our God, the Lord is One."[10]

Seven days later, on the New Moon of Sivan, the very day on
which [the children of] Israel had arrived at Sinai to receive the
Torah, those Jews who were in the court of the bishop were subjected to great anguish and the enemy dealt them what they had
dealt the others, tormenting them and putting them to the sword.

The Jews, inspired by the valor of their brethren who had sanctified the Name of their Creator, did likewise. They took their own lives; mothers were dashed to pieces with their children, fathers fell upon their sons and were slaughtered upon them. The enemy stripped them naked, dragged them along, and then cast them off. On this day of the New Moon a few were permitted to remain alive. The number of those slain for the sanctification of God's name during the two days was about eight hundred,[11] and they were all buried. It is of these that the Prophet Jeremiah lamented: "They that were brought up in scarlet embrace dunghills."[12]

There arose then a young man named Simḥa ha-Cohen. When he saw that they were bringing him to the house of their idolatry, he remained silent until he arrived there. When he arrived there, he drew a knife from his sleeve and slew a knight who was a nephew[13] of the bishop. They immediately cut his body to pieces. And it is of him and his like that it is said: "They that love Him shall be as the sun when it goes forth in its might."[14]

For these righteous people do I wail and lament bitterly:

I keen, mourn, and lament over the extolled community;
    In my heart there is wailing, for my wound is severe:
Clothed in horror is the sorrowful remnant,
    For the great diadem of gold has fallen from their head.
Friends and beloved ones, the wicked have consumed—
    My malevolent neighbors, who have struck at the heritage.
For these things do I mourn; for I became horrified.
    My eye is a fount of tears, and I weep day and night.
Loudly I utter a calamitous cry, for the children are come to birth;[15]
    Disaster upon disaster, utter extermination.
They have washed and cleansed themselves before You, as the re-
        cipients of Your word at Sinai,
    And called out Your Name, Lord, in defiance of the clamoring
        rabble.
In multitudes, in each region, they have sanctified my God, the King,
    Abiding now in the royal palace, in happiness and joy.
May the strength of their virtue, and their righteousness as well,
    Stand their survivors in good stead forever and ever, Selah.

On the third of the week, the third of the month of Sivan, a day of sanctification and abstinence for Israel in preparation for receiving the Torah—the community of Mainz, saints of the Most High, withdrew from each other in sanctity and purity, and sanctified themselves to ascend to God all together, young and old. Those who had been "pleasant in their lifetime . . . were not parted in death," for all of them were gathered in the courtyard of the bishop.

The enemy arose against them, killing little children and women, youth and old men, viciously—all on one day—a nation of fierce countenance that does not respect the old nor show favor to the young. The enemy showed no mercy for babes and sucklings, no pity for women about to give birth. They left no survivor or remnant but a dried date, and two or three pits,[16] for all of them had been eager to sanctify the Name of Heaven. And when the enemy was upon them, they all cried out in a great voice, with one heart and one tongue: "Hear, O Israel," etc.

Some of the pious old men wrapped themselves in their fringed prayer shawls and sat in the bishop's courtyard. They hastened to fulfill the will of their Creator, not wishing to flee just to be saved for temporal life, for lovingly they accepted Heaven's judgment. The foe hurled stones and arrows at them, but they did not scurry to flee. Women, too, girded their loins with strength and slew their own sons and daughters, and then themselves. Tenderhearted men also mustered their strength and slaughtered their wives, sons, daughters, and infants. The most gentle and tender of women slaughtered the child of her delight.

Let the ears hearing this and its like be seared, for who has heard or seen the likes of it? Did it ever occur that there were one thousand *'Akedot*[17] on a single day? The earth trembled over just one offering that occurred on the myrrh mountain.[18] Behold, the valiant ones cry without; the angels of peace weep bitterly.[19] But the heavens did not darken and the stars did not withhold their radiance! Why did not the sun and the moon turn dark, when one thousand three hundred holy souls were slain on a single day[20] — among them babes and sucklings who had not sinned or transgressed—the souls of innocent poor people? Wilt Thou restrain Thyself for these things, O Lord?

Sixty people were rescued on that day in the courtyard of the bishop. He took them to the villages of the Rheingau in order to save them. There, too, the enemy assembled against them and slew them all. For because of our sins, the slayer had been given permission to injure. Wherever a Jew would flee to save his soul—there the rock would cry out from the wall.[21]

Two pious men were spared on that day because the enemy had defiled them against their will. The name of one was Master Uri, and the name of the second was Master Isaac—the latter being accompanied by his two daughters. They, too, greatly sanctified the Name and now accepted upon themselves a death so awesome that it is not recorded in all Biblical admonitions. For on the eve of Pentecost, Isaac, the son of David, the *Parnass*, slaughtered his two daughters and set his house afire. Thereupon he and Master Uri went to the synagogue before the Holy Ark, and they both died there before the Lord, wholeheartedly yielding to the consuming flames. And it is of them and their like that it is written: "He who offers the sacrifice of thanksgiving honors Me."[22]

For the pious ones of Mainz I shall let out wailing like a jackal:

Woe is me for my calamity, severe is my wound, I declare:
"My tent has been pillaged and all my ropes have been broken: my
      children have left me."[23]

My heart goes out to the slain of Mainz, those valued as gold and as
      scarlet.
My heart ails for them while I must suppress my cries of woe,

Erudite as "the families of scribes that dwelt at Jabez: Tirathites,
      the Shimeathites, the Sucathites."[24] They were exterminated
      for my sins,
Being men that had wisdom and understanding to comprehend
      the Torah.

It is for them that I weep, that tears drop from my eye;
For the calamity of my people I am racked; darkness has descended,
      desolation has taken hold of me.

Elders have vanished from the gate; those who sound their voice to
      instruct me are no more.
This Torah—who will extol thee? Gone are those who were wont to
      utter your words in my ear!

Who will explain and teach me your esoteric knowledge and your
  curled locks?[25]
At the inception of the night vigils, arise, and mourn before your
  Master!
For the life of those who were wont to utter your words, allow
  yourself no rest.
Strive my soul, battle for me, O Lord, defend my case and right my
  wrong!
Avenge me, avenge the blood of Your Saints, O Lord, my Master,
For naught can take their place. You have assured and told me—
I will avenge their blood which I have not avenged; and my dwelling
  is in Zion.

As it is said: "And I will hold as innocent their blood which I have
not avenged; and the Lord dwelleth in Zion."[26] And it is said: "I
have set their blood upon the bare rock, that it should not be
covered."[27]

The news reached Cologne on the fifth of the month, the eve of
Pentecost, and instilled mortal fear into the community. Everyone
fled to the houses of Gentile acquaintances and remained there. On
the following morning the enemies rose up and broke into the
houses, looting and plundering. The foe destroyed the synagogue
and removed the Torah Scrolls, desecrating them and casting them
into the streets to be trodden underfoot. On the very day that the
Torah was given, when the earth trembled and its pillars quivered,
they now tore, burned, and trod upon it—those wicked evildoers
regarding whom it is said: "Robbers have entered and profaned
it."[28]

O God, will You not punish them for these acts? How long will
You look on at the wicked and remain silent? "See, O Lord, and
behold, how abject I am become."[29]

That very day they shed the blood of a pious man named Isaac.
The enemy led him to their house of idolatry, but he spat at them,
reviled and ridiculed them. Isaac did not desire to flee from his
home, for he was happy and eager to accept the judgment of
Heaven. They also slew a pious woman.

The rest were saved in the homes of acquaintances to which they had fled, until the bishop took them to his villages on the tenth of the month, to save them, and dispersed them in the seven villages. There they remained until the month of Tammuz, anticipating death each day. They fasted daily, even on the two consecutive festive days of the New Moon of Tammuz, which that year occurred on Monday and Tuesday. They also fasted the following day.

On that day, the enemies marked with insignia [i.e., the Crusaders], as well as those unmarked, came, for it was St. John's day. They all gathered in the village of Neuss. Samuel, the son of Asher, sanctified God's Name for all to behold, as did his two sons who were with him. After he and his sons were slain, they [the Crusaders] defiled their bodies by dragging them through the muddy streets and trampling them. Then they hanged his sons at the entrance to his home in order to mock him. "How long, O Lord, will You be angry," etc.[30] "How long, O God, shall the adversary reproach," etc.[31] "For these things I weep; mine eye, mine eye runneth down with water."[32]

The following day the enemies again rose up, and the pious men of the village of Wevelinghofen were slain. They, too, greatly sanctified the Name—Levi, son of Samuel, his wife and children, and his entire household, the aged Mistress Rachel, wife of Solomon ha-Cohen, and the entire group which Levi had brought there with him: men, women, and children, grooms and brides, old men and women, who slaughtered themselves and exposed their throats for their heads to be severed in sanctification of the One Name. This happened in the ponds around the village.[33]

There was a pious man there of ripe old age by the name of Rabbi Samuel, son of Yehiel. He had an only son, a handsome young man, whose appearance was like Lebanon. They fled together into the water, and the youth stretched out his neck to his father for slaughter as they stood in the waters. The father recited the benediction for Ritual Slaughter over him, and the son answered, "Amen." All those standing around them responded in a loud voice: "Hear, O Israel, the Lord is our God, the Lord is One!"

Behold, all ye mortals, the great valor of the son who, though not bound, submitted himself to slaughter, and how great was the fortitude of the father, who was not softened by pity for so pleasant and handsome a youth. Who will hear and not weep? The offering and he who offered him up were unanimous in their desire that their life-breath be stilled. It is of them and the likes of them that it is said: "He who offers the sacrifice of thanksgiving honors Me."[34]

What did the aged father now do? There was a young man with them, a God-fearing man, the synagogue sexton, called Menaḥem. The old man said to him: "Here, brave Menaḥem, take my sword and slaughter me with my pious son." The youth summoned up courage, took the sword, and slaughtered the pious old man with his son. Master Menaḥem then threw himself on the sword and he, too, died there.

Thus these saints sanctified the Name of their Creator. Many there were who acted thus, sanctifying the Name of Heaven openly. Truly, the eye has seen and given witness, the ear has heard and attested to it. There were also some who drowned themselves in the waters, and nothing remained but three seeds.

On the third of the month, the pious people of the village of Eller[35] were slain. Not more than a few remained and they, too, greatly sanctified the Name. There was a pious man there named Isaac the Levite, whom they subjected to great torture, defiling him against his will, as he was unable to resist, being senseless from their beatings. He later regained consciousness, and three days later he returned to his home in Cologne, lingered there a short while, and then went to the Rhine River and drowned himself. It is of him and the likes of him that it is said: "I will bring back from Bashan, I will bring them back from the depths of the sea."[36]

On the fourth of the month, which was Sabbath Eve, the enemy gathered against the saints of Eller to torment them cruelly, so that they would submit to their defilement. When the people learned of this, they gathered in one chamber and confessed to their Creator. The devout agreed to slaughter all those present. There were about three hundred souls in that city.

These are the names of the devout ones who consented to slay the others: Gershom; Judah, son of Abraham, and his brother Joseph; Judah, the Levite, son of Rabbi Samuel; and Peter.[37] They took hold of their swords, sealed the doors, and slaughtered all those present. Peter then slaughtered the other four and, going up onto a tower, threw himself down to the ground and perished before God.

From amongst all those people, only two young men and two babes remained; their windpipes had been slit, but they survived.

On that very day the calamity reached the pious men of Xanten. The enemy attacked and slew them just as the Sabbath was setting in. There were some saintly individuals there who were ushering in the Sabbath at the very moment of slaughter.

As a man rejoices when he finds booty, so were they joyous and eager to serve our God and sanctify His Name, and thus did they, too, sanctify Him by their sacrifices.

There was a pious man there, called "the Rabbi from France," who said to them: "Thus do we do it in our place." He dug out some earth, recited the Ritual Slaughter blessing, slaughtered himself, and thus expired before the Lord. All the others called out, "Hear, O Israel," etc., in a great voice. Not one of them survived, except those discovered in the morning critically wounded among the dead. All who perished were brought to burial.

On the seventh of Tammuz, the enemies arose against the poor and oppressed people in the town of Mehr. There besieged the city a multitude as numerous as the grains of sand upon the seashore. The mayor of the city went out to meet them and requested they wait in the field outside the city until daybreak. He spoke thus: "Perhaps I can coax the Jews to do as I desire." This found favor in their eyes, and those besieging the city on account of the Jews therein withdrew. The mayor did not despair, and had the Jews summoned and brought before him, and he said to them: "Hearken to me, O Jews. I originally vowed to you that I would shelter and protect you as long as there was a single Jew alive in the world. And as I pledged, so have I done. Henceforth, however, I cannot do anything to save you from all these nations. Decide now what you wish to do. Know that if you do not do thus-and-so, the city will be destroyed; and I would rather give you over into their hands than have them besiege the city and destroy the fortress."

Young and old, they all replied: "Behold we are ready to extend our throats to die attesting the fear of our Creator and the Oneness of His Name." When the mayor saw that he was unable to sway them, he immediately tried another ploy and led them to the outskirts of the city, to the site where the errant ones were encamped.

Those thus seized were left there, and their captors returned to the city, their swords having been covered with the blood of animals and beasts, in order to deceive those remaining into believing that the others had been slain. They did all this in order to intimidate them into complying with their wish by soiling and defiling themselves in their profane waters. However, all this was to no effect and of no avail, for they declared in unison: "We have no desire for your dogma."

When they [the mayor and the burghers] saw that their ploy was to no effect, they returned them to the city and imprisoned them, each one separately, until the morrow, so that they would not slay each other, as they heard that the others had done.

There were two pious women there, Mistress Gentile and Mistress Rebecca; one had gone into labor and given birth to a male child, while the other, in her great fear, had caught a fever, and they were both ill. A very beautiful girl was also there with them. When they saw that the enemies had arisen against them, they slaughtered the pretty girl, who was only ten years old. They also took hold of the tender child who had been born that week, compassionately wrapped him in his swaddling clothes, and cast him down from the tower in which they were imprisoned.

When the foe saw what the Jews had done, they took counsel against them. The following day they seized all of them and dragged them to the errant ones. They slew some of them and forcibly defiled those whom they permitted to live, and they had their way with them.

A pious man by the name of Shemariah was promised by the bursar of the bishop, who was an acquaintance of his, that he would take him along and save him in return for money which he had given him. He led Shemariah, his wife, and their three sons through the forest until the fifteenth day of the month of Av.[38] He led them this way and that, and detained them here and there, and he pressed them until Shemariah sent to his sons in Speyer for money. His sons dispatched a *zakuk* of gold; upon getting the money, he immediately took them and handed them over to the enemy in the village of Tremonia.[39]

When Shemariah arrived there, the villagers rejoiced, for they recognized him. The townspeople agreed to the request of the Jews to wait until the next day and then do as they desired. They immediately made a merry feast, and [Shemariah and his family] ate with them while still conforming to the laws of ritually permissible food and, in purity, using a new knife,[40] [for they] said: "While we yet adhere to our faith, we desire to act in accordance with our custom; tomorrow we will all be one people. Now place us in one room until tomorrow, for we are weary and tired from the road." The villagers granted their request.

Shemariah arose in the night, girded his loins, and slaughtered his wife and children. He tried to slaughter himself, too, but fainted and did not die. The first thing the next morning, the villagers came, thinking they would find what Shemariah had promised; instead, they found him in this condition.

They said to him: "Although you have acted in a defiant manner, your life shall be spared if you adopt our erroneous belief. Otherwise, we will inflict a violent death upon you, burying you alive with those you have slain." He answered: "Heaven forfend that I should deny the Living God for a dead, decaying carcass."

They dug the grave, and Shemariah entered under his own power. He laid his sons on his left and his wife on his right. They threw earth upon him, asking from time to time: "Have you changed your mind yet?" He disregarded their challenge to believe in their contamination. They did this repeatedly, uncovering him from time to time to see if he would change his mind or not; but he disregarded them. Finally, they angrily threw the earth upon him, ignoring his cries. His voice was heard throughout that entire day, but they made jest of him.

Wilt Thou restrain Thyself for these things, O Lord? We have experienced all the admonitions, those enumerated in Scripture as well as those unwritten, and our souls are greatly frightened. How long will You be angry with us, O Lord; how long will You draw out Your anger from generation to generation?

In the village of Kerpen, they had their way with the Jews living there, defiling them with their profane waters and abusing them. Wilt Thou restrain Thyself for these things, O Lord?

They did the same in the city of Geldern. The Jews were subjected to plundering and abuse, and there was no one to rescue them. "For these things I weep; mine eye, mine eye runneth down with water."[41]

There are two Ellers where Jewish martyrs were slain. The first was a village close to Julich, and the other is the city on its present known site.[42] On the eighth of Iyar, the saints of Speyer were slain. On the twenty-fourth of that month, some of the community of Worms were killed; it was on the New Moon of Sivan that the enemy slew, not leaving a single survivor among them. On the third of Sivan, the holy community of Mainz were slain. In the Cologne region they began to slay and defile on Pentecost, until the eighth of Tammuz.[43] All these persecutions occurred in the year [4]856 [1096].

For the pious ones of Cologne let the daughters of Israel go and wail,
    make great lamentation and keening,
For a holy, worthy, esteemed community, all of whose deeds were
    done in faithfulness.
To her do I devote mourning, lamentation, like the ostriches,
For who can withhold his words for the holy community, pure
    as a one-year-old child?
Their deeds were righteous in the eyes of Him-Who-Dwells-in-
    Heaven;
Performers of meritorious deeds and charitable works, beyond
    limit or reckoning.
Therefore, summon the husbandman[44] to mourning, those skilled
    in elegy to make lament,
And wail in the streets and in the marketplaces, mourn everywhere.
For she sacrificed her life, and adhered to the fear of her Master;
Her blood has congealed like the wine of Senir and Hermon,[45]
And they sanctified the Name of the Holy-One-Who-Dwells-in-
    Heaven.
On hearing such tidings let me cry out like a swallow and a crane,
    and moan like a dove.
And may He judge their blood, causing many to be slain, with great
    wrath, without mercy!

For the sacred community of Cologne let me raise my voice in bitter
    lament:

For those who have martyred themselves in sanctification of the
    Name let me wail and wander about to all the cities,
And clothe myself in sack and ashes, and drink bitter water;
And go to sing songs of lament on the mountains.[46]
And let all the survivors mourn and grieve, all pure hearts,
For the holy community let them mourn forever.
May their death be a source of forgiveness and pardon for us.
Prepare hastily[47] mourning and wailing for the pious of Cologne.

Let me raise my voice in lament, weep and mourn for the calamity
    that has befallen,
How dear they were to me! My entrails are seared for Your dear
    ones, O God!
The gold has become dimmed, the gilded sapphire altered and
    darkened, no longer to be beheld.
Warriors with high hand entered their gates, they who cultivated
    wisdom
Were torn by the wolves who have devoured and displaced them,
    rendered them desolate;
They have trodden upon her [the community at Cologne] flesh,
    inflicting injury, lesion, and fresh wound.
My eyes have been depleted, flowing with tears, crying and weeping;
Weak is my spirit, as I wail with my words and I moan with lament
For the lives of my blossoms, the babes I have raised, who were
    bound to be offered before God;
Compassionate women, in tears, with their own hands slaughtered,
    as at the 'Akedah of Moriah.
Innocent souls withdrew to eternal life, to their station on high.
Let not Your foes triumph! Let the martyr's blood spatter Your
    royal purple.[48]
Cast down their triumph and pour out the lifeblood of the enemy,
    may it be dashed against a purple garment.[49]
Array their defeat, crush the winepress, with Your outstretched
    arm!

As it is said: "And I trod down the peoples in Mine Anger," etc. And
it is said: "I have trodden the winepress," etc.[50]
    And as the foes had done in these communities, so did they do
in others—in the cities of Trier, Metz, Regensburg, and Prague.[51]

The Jews sanctified the Holy Name with love and devotion, completing their task by evening.[52] It was all at one time, from the month of Iyar till the month of Tammuz, that they ascended to God in sanctity and purity.

These were the potters, who dwelt among plantations; there they dwelt, occupied in the work of the King[53] for Whose sake they gave their lives. May He requite their deeds unto them and provide them with their reward according to the work of their hands. Their souls are bound in the bond of life in the King's sanctuary. Each of them is garbed in the eight vestments of clouds of glory;[54] each crowned with two diadems, one of precious stones and pearls and one of fine gold; and each bearing eight myrtles in his hand. Each is the object of adulation, being told: "Go thy way, eat thy bread with joy."[55]

This is all expounded in the Midrash on the verse: "Oh how abundant is Thy goodness, which Thou has laid up for them that fear Thee."[56]

May their merit stand us in good stead forever, Selah, to hasten the time of redemption speedily and soon.

Amen, may it so be His will.

The Narrative of the Old Persecutions, or *Mainz Anonymous*

INTRODUCTION

Because of its narrator's heavy emphasis on Mainz, *The Narrative of the Old Persecutions*[1] is also known as the *Mainz Anonymous*. The author of this chronicle is unknown and the narrative itself yields no clue to either its date or its place of origin. Its chronological place among the Hebrew chronicles of the First Crusade is debatable.

On the one hand, the libel of well-poisoning, unique to this chronicle, is indicative of the later Middle Ages. In addition, the very character of the script suggests the style of the fourteenth-century German scribes. On the other hand, it has been proposed that the fragmentary nature of the manuscript, rather than indicating derivation from the more complete Bar Simson chronicle, reveals a faithfulness to the parent source of all three which is lost to us today.[2]

The *Mainz Anonymous* chronicle is distinct from the Bar Simson and Bar Nathan chronicles in several respects. First, the Mainz is our sole record of letters of warning sent from France to the German communities. The anonymous chronicler, in describing the complacency of the Rhenish Jews ("All the communities have decreed a fast day. We have done our duty. . . . As for ourselves, there is no great cause for fear"), reveals a more realistic grasp of the Jews' circumstances than does any of the other chronicles. The Rhenish Jew of pre-Crusade Europe was confident of his own socioeconomic status and placed great faith in the protection of the emperor and in the privileges granted by him. Despite the fact that

95

The opening pages of the only extant manuscript of the *Mainz Anonymous*, dating from 1560 and copied from an earlier manuscript. (Courtesy of Hessische Landes-und Hochschulbibliothek, Darmstadt.)

the Jews of Worms hear of the murders committed in Speyer, some
do not even flee to the bishop but rather place their faith in the
good will of the burghers. In contrast to this initial display of hopeful trust and assurance,
the anonymous chronicler makes clear mention of the subsequent
betrayal of German communities at the hands of the bishop,
burghers, and nobility. The Jews of Mainz despair when they hear
the news of Speyer and Worms, and they turn to the bishop for help.
The bishop, his ministers, servants, and great noblemen counsel the
Jews to bring their money to the church treasury and their families
to the courtyard, where they are again betrayed. In this instance the
chronicler manifests a change in attitude toward the bishop and his
belief that the bishop had once intended to extend his good will to
the Jews. A similar change in attitude appears in Bar Simson's
chronicle, in which the narrator's initial trust of the Christian clergy
is shattered by subsequent events.

Second, as mentioned above, the incidence of the libel of well-
poisoning is unique to the *Mainz Anonymous*, perhaps indicating
authorship even as late as the Black Plague of the fourteenth
century, a period rife with libels of this type. Nevertheless, any attempt at dating the manuscript based upon this accusation is to be
taken with reservation.[3]

The *Mainz Anonymous* is noteworthy for its detailed treatment
of an act of retribution, an offensive, rather than a defensive act,
which is mentioned, more briefly, only in Eliezer bar Nathan's
chronicle. This is the episode of Simha ha-Cohen, a young man who
swears to submit to baptism if he can see the bishop. While awaiting
the rite in the bishop's couryard, he draws a knife to murder the
bishop's nephew and two others. He is, of course, finally slain.

Interestingly enough, in describing the activities of the Crusader
groups, the narrator restricted himself to the deeds of Emicho, without mention of either Peter the Hermit or the Hungarian demise as
recounted in Bar Simson. Nevertheless, mention is made of a certain
Dithmar,[4] found nowhere else in the Hebrew chronicles. These
added accounts, unique to the *Mainz Anonymous*, make it a valuable
complement to the companion chronicles of Bar Simson and Bar
Nathan in relating the history of the Jews during the First Crusade.

The
Narrative of
the Old Persecutions,
or
Mainz Anonymous

I shall begin the narrative of past persecution—may the Lord protect us and all of Israel from future persecution.

In the year one thousand twenty-eight[1] after the destruction of the Temple, this evil befell Israel. The noblemen and counts and the common people in the land of France united and decided to soar up like an eagle,[2] to wage war, and to clear a way to Jerusalem, the Holy City, and to come to the tomb of the crucified one, a rotting corpse that cannot avail and cannot save, being of no worth or significance.

They said to each other: "Look now, we are going to a distant country to make war against mighty kings and are endangering our lives to conquer the kingdoms which do not believe in the crucified one, when actually it is the Jews who murdered and crucified him." They stirred up hatred against us in all quarters and declared that either we should accept their abominable faith or else they would annihilate us all, even infants and sucklings. The noblemen and common people placed an evil symbol—a vertical line over a horizontal one—on their garments and special hats on their heads.

When the communities in the land of France[3] heard this, they were gripped by fear and trembling, and they resorted to the custom of their ancestors.[4] They wrote letters and dispatched messengers to all communities around the River Rhine, bidding them to proclaim fastdays and seek mercy from God, that He might save them from hands of the enemy. When the letters reached the saints, the men of renown, the pillars of the universe in Mainz, they wrote to the land of France, saying: "All the communities have decreed a fastday. We have done our duty. May the Omnipresent One save us and you from all the trouble and affliction. We are greatly concerned about your well-being. As for ourselves, there is no great cause for fear. We have not heard a word of such matters, nor has it been hinted that our lives are threatened by the sword.[5]

When the errant ones started arriving in this land [Rhineland], they sought money to buy bread. We gave it to them, applying to ourselves the verse: "Serve the king of Babylon, and live."[6] All this, however, did not avail us. Because of our sins, whenever the errant ones arrived at a city, the local burghers would harass us, for they were at one with them in their intention to destroy vine and root[7] all along their way to Jerusalem.

When the errant ones came, battalion after battalion like the army of Sennacherib,[8] some of the noblemen in this kingdom declared: "Why do we sit? Let us join them, for every man who goes on this path and clears the way to the unholy grave of the crucified one will be fully qualified and ready for Hell."[9] The errant ones gathered, the nobles and the commoners from all provinces, until they were as numerous as the sands of the sea. A proclamation was issued: "Whosoever kills a Jew will receive pardon for all his sins."[10] There was a Count Dithmar[11] there who said that he would not depart from this kingdom until he had slain one Jew; only then would he proceed on his journey.

When the holy community of Mainz learned of this, they decreed a fastday and cried out loudly to the Lord. Young and old alike fasted day and night, reciting prayers of lamentation in the morning and evening. Despite all of this, however, our God did not withhold His wrath from us. For the errant ones came with their insignia and banners before our homes, and, upon seeing one of us, they would pursue and pierce him with their lances—till we became afraid even to step on the thresholds of our homes.

On the eighth of Iyar, on the Sabbath, the measure of justice began to fall upon us. The errant ones and the burghers first plotted against the holy men, the saints of the Most High, in Speyer, and they planned to seize all of them together in the synagogue. Told of this, the saints arose on Sabbath morning, prayed quickly, and departed from the synagogue. When the enemy saw that their plot to take them all captive together had been frustrated, they rose up against them and slew eleven of them. This was the beginning of the persecution, fulfilling the Biblical verse: "And at my sanctuary shall you begin."[12]

When Bishop John[13] heard of this, he came with a large army and wholeheartedly aided the community, taking them indoors and rescuing them from the enemy. The bishop then took some of the burghers and cut off their hands, for he was a righteous man among the Gentiles, and the Omnipresent One used him as a means for our benefit and rescue.

Rabbi Moshe, the *Parnass*, son of Rabbi Yekuthiel, stood in the breach. He endangered himself for his fellow Jews.[14] As a result of his efforts, all those who had been forcibly converted and had survived in Henry's domain by fleeing to various places were enabled to return.[15] And through the aid of the king, Bishop John enabled the remnant of the community of Speyer to take refuge in his fortified towns.

The Lord had mercy upon them for the sake of His Great Name, and the bishop concealed them until the enemies of the Name had passed. The Jews engaged in fasting, weeping, and lamentation, and began to despair greatly, for day after day the errant ones and the Gentiles and Emicho, may his bones be ground to dust, and the common people all gathered against them to capture and annihilate them. Through the efforts of Rabbi Moshe, the *Parnass*, Bishop John saved them, for the Lord had moved him to keep them alive without taking a bribe—for it was the Lord's doing to grant us a vestige and a remnant by the bishop's hand.

When the bad tidings reached Worms[16] that some of the community of Speyer had been murdered, the Jews of Worms cried out to the Lord and wept in great and bitter lamentation. They saw that the decree had been issued in Heaven and that there was no escape and no recourse. The community then was divided into two groups: some fled to the bishop and sought refuge in his castles; others remained in their homes, for the burghers had given them false promises, which, like broken reedstaffs, cause harm and do no good.[17] For the burghers were in league with the errant ones in their intention to wipe out our people's name and remnant. So they offered us false solace: "Do not fear them, for anyone who kills one of you—his life will be forfeit for yours." The Jews had nowhere to flee, as the Jewish community had entrusted all their money to their non-Jewish neighbors. It was for this very reason that their neighbors handed them over to the enemy.

On the tenth day of Iyar, a Monday, they cunningly plotted against the Jews. They took a rotting corpse of theirs, which had been buried thirty days previously, and bore it into the city, saying: "Look what the Jews have done to one of us. They took a Gentile, boiled him in water, and poured the water into our wells in order to poison us to death!"[18] When the errant ones and burghers heard this, they cried out. They all assembled, anyone capable of drawing and bearing a sword, big and small, and declared: "Behold, the time has come to avenge him who was nailed to the wood, whom their forefathers slew. Now, let no remnant or vestige of them be allowed to escape, not even a babe or a suckling in the cradle."

The enemy came and smote those who had remained at home— handsome lads, pretty and pleasant girls, old men and old women— all extended their necks in martyrdom. Manumitted servants and maids[19] were also slain in sanctification of the Eternally Awesome and Sublime Name of Him Who rules above and below, Who was and will be, Whose Name is Lord of Hosts, and Who is crowned with the graces of the Seventy-Two Names,[20] He Who created the Torah nine hundred and seventy-four generations before the creation of the world; and there were twenty-six generations between the creation and Moses,[21] father of the prophets, through whom the Torah was given—the same Moses who wrote in this Torah: "It is the Lord Whom you have chosen today," etc.[22] It was for Him and His Torah that they were slain like oxen, and dragged through the marketplaces and streets like sheep to be slaughtered, and lay naked in the streets, for the foe stripped them and left them naked.

When the survivors saw their brethren lying naked and the chaste daughters of Israel naked—under this great duress they yielded to the foe. For the errant ones had said that they would not leave a single survivor. So some of the Jews said: "Let us do their will for the time being, and then go and bury our brethren[23] and also save our children from them." For the enemy had already seized the few remaining children, thinking that perhaps they would be gained for their erroneous faith. But the children did not turn away from their Creator, and their hearts did not stray after the crucified one; but they clung to God-on-High.

Those of the community who had remained within the bishop's chambers sent garments so that the dead might be clothed by those rescued, for the survivors were charitable people. The heads of the community remained there [in the bishop's palace], and most of the community were spared initially. They sent words of comfort to the forced converts: "Do not fear and do not take to heart what you have done. If the Blessed Holy One saves us from our enemies, then we shall be with you in death and in life. But do not turn away from the Lord."

On the twenty-third of Iyar, the errant ones and the burghers said: "Let us also take vengeance against those who have remained in the courtyard and chambers of the bishop." People assembled from all the surrounding villages, together with the errant ones and the burghers, and they besieged and fought against them. A great battle was fought between the two groups until they captured the chambers where the children of the Sacred Covenant were sheltered. When they saw that the war was on every side by decree of the King of Kings, they justified Heaven's judgment upon them, placed their trust in their Creator, and offered true sacrifices, taking their children and wholeheartedly slaughtering them in witness to the Oneness of the Venerated and Awesome Name. The notables of the community were slain there.

There was a man there by the name of Meshullam, son of Isaac, and he called out in a great voice to his beloved wife Mistress Zipporah and to all those present: "Hear me, adults and children! God gave me this son; my wife Zipporah bore him in her advanced age. His name is Isaac. I shall now offer him up as a sacrifice as our Father Abraham did his son Isaac." His wife Zipporah said to him: "My lord, my lord, wait, do not yet move your hand toward the boy whom I have raised and brought up, whom I bore in my old age. Slaughter me first and let me not see the death of the child."[24] He replied: "I shall not tarry even for a second. He Who gave him to us shall take him as His share and place him in the bosom of our Father Abraham." He bound Isaac, his son, and took the knife in his hand to slaughter him, reciting the blessing for Ritual Slaughter. The boy responded: "Amen." And he slaughtered the boy. He took his shrieking wife and together they left the room. The errant ones then slew them.

"Wilt Thou restrain Thyself for these things, O Lord?"[25] Yet, with all this, His great wrath did not turn away from us!

There was a lad there named Isaac, son of Daniel. They asked him: "Do you wish to exchange your God for a disgusting idol?" He replied, "God forbid that I should deny Him. In Him I shall place my trust and I shall even yield up my soul to Him." They put a rope around his neck and dragged him through the entire city in the muddy streets to the house of their idolatry. There was still some life in his frame when they said to him: "You can still be saved if you agree to change your religion." Having already been strangled, he could not utter a word from his mouth, so he gestured with his finger to say: "Cut off my head." And they slit his throat.

There was yet another youth there [in Worms], by the name of Simḥa ha-Cohen, son of our Master Isaac ha-Cohen,[26] whom they sought to contaminate with their putrid water. They said to him: "Look, they have all been killed already and are lying naked." The youth cleverly answered: "I will do all that you ask of me if you take me to the bishop." So they took him and brought him to the bishop's courtyard. The bishop's nephew was there, too, and they began to invoke the name of the foul and disgusting scion and then left him in the bishop's courtyard. The youth drew his knife, then gnashed his teeth, like a lion worrying his prey,[27] at the nobleman, the bishop's kinsman; then he dashed at him and plunged the knife into his belly, and the man fell dead. Turning from there, he stabbed yet another two, until the knife broke in his hand. They fled in all directions. When they saw that his knife had broken, they attacked him and slew him. There was slain the youth who had sanctified the Name, doing what the rest of the community had not done—slaying three uncircumcised ones with his knife.

The rest devotedly fasted daily and then endured martyrdom. They had wept for their families and their friends to the point of exhaustion, so that they were unable to fight against the enemy. They declared: "It is the decree of the King. Let us fall into the

hand of the Lord, and let us go and behold the Great Light." There
they all fell attesting the Oneness of the Name.

A distinguished woman, named Mistress Mina, found refuge
below the ground in a house outside the city. The people of the city
gathered outside her hiding place and called: "Behold, you are a
woman of valor. Perceive that God is no longer concerned with
saving you, for the slain are lying naked in the open streets with no
one to bury them. Yield to baptism." They fell all over themselves
entreating her, as they did not wish to slay her, for her fame had
traveled far because the notables of her city and the nobles of the
land used to frequent her company. But she answered by saying:
"Heaven forfend that I should deny God-on-High. Slay me for Him
and His Holy Torah, and do not tarry any longer." There she was
slain, she who was praised in the gates.[28] They all were slain sanctifying the Name wholeheartedly and willingly, slaughtering one
another: young men and maidens, old men and women, and babes,
too, were sacrificed in sanctification of the Name.

Those specifically mentioned by name acted thus, and the
others not mentioned by name even surpassed them in valor. What
they did had never been witnessed by the eye of man. It is of them
and the likes of them that it was said: "From mortals, by Your
hand, O Lord; from mortals of this world, whose portion is in this
life. . . ."[29] "Neither hath the eye seen a God beside Thee, Who
worketh for him that waiteth for Him."[30] They all fell by the hand
of the Lord and returned to their rest, to the Great Light in the
Garden of Eden.[31] Behold, their souls are bound up till the time of
the End[32] in the bond of life with the Lord, God, Who created them.

When the saints, the pious ones of the Most High, the holy community of Mainz, heard that some of the community of Speyer had
been slain and that the community of Worms had been attacked a
second time, their spirits failed and their hearts melted and became
as water. They cried out to the Lord: "Alas, O Lord, God! Will You
completely annihilate the remnant of Israel? Where are all your
wonders which our forefathers related to us, saying: 'Did You not
bring us up from Egypt, O Lord?' But now You have forsaken us,
delivering us into the hands of the Gentiles to destroy us!"

All the Jewish community leaders assembled and came before

the bishop with his officers and servants, and said to them: "What shall we do about the news we have received regarding the slaughter of our brethren in Speyer and Worms?" They [the bishop and his followers] replied: "Heed our advice and bring all your money into our treasury and into the treasury of the bishop. And you, your wives, sons, and all your belongings shall come into the courtyard of the bishop. Thus will you be saved from the errant ones." Actually, they gave this advice so as to herd us together and hold us like fish that are caught in an evil net and then turn us over to the enemy.[33] The bishop assembled his ministers, servants, and great noblemen in order to rescue us from the errant ones, for at first it had been his desire to save us, but in the end he turned against us.[34]

One day a Gentile woman came, bringing a goose which she had raised since it was newborn. The goose would accompany the Gentile woman wherever she went, and the woman would call to all passersby, saying: "Look, the goose understands my intention to go straying and he desires to accompany me."[35] The errant ones and burghers then gathered against us and said to us: "Where is He in Whom you place your trust? How will you be saved? See the wonders which the crucified one works for us." And they all came with swords and lances to destroy us, but some of the burghers came and prevented them.[36] At this point, the errant ones all united and battled the burghers on the bank of the River Rhine, until a Crusader was slain.

Seeing this the Crusaders cried out: "The Jews have caused this," and nearly all of them reassembled.

When the holy people saw this, their hearts melted. The foe reviled and derided them, with the intention of falling upon them. Upon hearing their words, the Jews, old and young alike, said: "Would that our death might be by the hand of the Lord, so that we should not perish at the hands of the enemies of the Lord; for He is a Merciful God, the sole sovereign of the universe."

They abandoned their houses; neither did they go to the synagogue save on the Sabbath. That was the final Sabbath before the evil decree befell us, when a small number of them entered the synagogue to pray; Rabbi Judah, son of Rabbi Isaac, also came there to pray on that Sabbath. They wept exceedingly, to the point of exhaustion, for they saw that it was a decree of the King of Kings. A venerable student, Baruch, son of Isaac, was there, and he said to us: "Know that this decree has been issued against us in truth and honesty, and we cannot be saved; for this past night I and my son-in-law Judah heard the souls praying here [in the synagogue] in a loud voice, like weeping.[37] When we heard the sound, we thought at first that perhaps some of the community had come back from the court of the bishop to pray in the synagogue at midnight because of their anguish and bitterness of heart. We ran to the door of the synagogue, but it was closed. We heard the sound, but we understood nothing. We returned frightened to our house, for it was close to the synagogue. Upon hearing this, we cried out: 'Alas, O Lord, God! Will You completely annihilate the remnant of Israel?'" Then they went and reported the occurrence to their brethren who were concealed in the court of the count and in the bishop's chambers. Thereupon, they, too, wept exceedingly.

On the New Moon of Sivan, the wicked Emicho, may his bones be ground to dust between iron millstones,[38] arrived outside the city with a mighty horde of errant ones and peasants, for he, too, had said: "I desire to follow the stray course." He was the chief of all our oppressors. He showed no mercy to the aged or youths, or maidens, babes, or sucklings—not even the sick; and he made the people of the Lord like dust to be trodden underfoot,[39] killing their young men by the sword and disemboweling their pregnant women.

They [the Crusaders] encamped outside the city for two days. The leaders of the community now said: "Let us send him money and give him letters of safe conduct, so that the communities along the route will honor him.[40] Perhaps the Lord will intercede in His abundant grace." For they had already given away their money, giving the bishop, the count, his officers and servants, and the burghers about four hundred halves[41] to aid them [the Jews]. But it was of no avail whatever.

We were not even comparable to Sodom and Gomorrah, for in their case they were offered reprieve if they could produce at least ten righteous people, whereas in our case not twenty, not even ten, were sought.

On the third of the month of Sivan, the day on which Moses said: "Be ready against the third day"[42] —on that day the diadem of Israel fell. The students of the Torah fell, and the outstanding scholars passed away; ended was the glory of the Torah, and the radiance of wisdom came to an end. "He hath cast down from heaven unto the earth the splendor of Israel."[43] Humility and the fear of sin ceased. Gone were the men of virtuous deed and purity, nullifiers of evil decrees and placaters of the wrath of their Creator.[44] Diminished were the ranks of those who give charity in secret;[45] gone was truth; gone were the explicators of the Word and the Law; fallen were the people of eminence, while the number of the shameless and insolent increased. Alas that they are gone! For since that day on which the Second Temple was destroyed, their like had not arisen, nor shall there be their like again. They sanctified the Name with all their heart and with all their soul and with all their might, happy are they.

At midday, the evil Emicho, may his bones be ground to dust, came with his entire horde. The townspeople opened the gate to him, and the enemies of the Lord said to one another: "Look, the gate has opened by itself; this the crucified one has done for us in order that we may avenge his blood on the Jews." They then came with their banners to the bishop's gate, where the people of the Sacred Covenant were assembled—a vast horde of them, as the sand upon the seashore. When the saints, the fearers of the Most High, saw this great multitude, they placed their trust in their Creator and clung to Him. They donned their armor and their weapons of war, adults and children alike, with Rabbi Kalonymos, son of Rabbi Meshullam, at their head.[46]

There was a pious man there, one of the great men of the generation, Rabbi Menaḥem, son of Rabbi David, the Levite. He said to the entire community: "Sanctify the Venerable and Awesome Name with a willing heart." They all answered as did the sons of our Father Jacob when he wished to reveal the time of the Final Redemption to his children but was prevented from doing so because the Divine Presence departed from him.[47] Jacob then said: "Perhaps I have been found to have a defect, just like Abraham, my grandfather, or like my father Isaac." And like our fathers, who, when they received the Torah at Mount Sinai at this season, promptly declared: "We shall do and obey,"[48] so did the martyrs now declare in a great voice: "Hear, O Israel, the Lord is our God, the Lord is One."

And they all advanced toward the gate to fight against the errant ones and the burghers. The two sides fought against each other around the gate, but as a result of their transgressions the enemy overpowered them and captured the gate. The bishop's people, who had promised to help them, being as broken reedstaffs, were the first to flee, so as to cause them to fall into the hands of the enemy.

The enemies now came into the courtyard and found Rabbi Isaac, son of Rabbi Moses, whom they smote with a stroke of the sword, slaying him. However, fifty-three souls fled with Rabbi Kalonymos via the bishop's chambers, entered a long chamber called the sacristy, and remained there. The enemy entered the courtyard on the third day of Sivan, the third day of the week, a day of darkness and gloom, a day of clouds and thick darkness—let darkness and the shadow of death claim it for their own, let God not inquire after it from above, nor let the light shine upon it. O Sun and Moon! Why did you not withhold your light? O stars, to whom Israel has been compared, and the twelve constellations, like the number of the tribes of Israel, the sons of Jacob—why was your light not withheld from shining for the enemy who sought to eradicate the name of Israel? Inquire and seek: was there ever such a mass sacrificial offering since the time of Adam?

When the people of the Sacred Covenant saw that the Heavenly decree had been issued and that the enemy had defeated them, they all cried out, young and old men, maidens, girls, children, menservants and maids, and wept for themselves and for their lives, saying: "Let us bear the yoke of the Holy Creed, for now the enemy can slay us but by the lightest of the four deaths, which is the sword,[49] and we shall then merit eternal life, and our souls will abide in the Garden of Eden, in the speculum of the Great Luminary." They all then said with gladness of heart and with willing soul: "After all things, there is no questioning the ways of the Holy One, blessed be He and blessed be His Name, Who has given us His Torah and has commanded us to allow ourselves to be killed and slain in witness to the Oneness of His Holy Name. Happy are we if we fulfill

His will, and happy is he who is slain or slaughtered and who dies attesting the Oneness of His Name. Such a one will not only be worthy of entering the World-to-Come and of sitting in the realm of the saints who are the pillars of the universe;[50] he will also exchange a world of darkness for one of light, a world of sorrow for one of joy, a transitory world for an eternal world."

And in a great voice they all cried out as one: "We need tarry no longer, for the enemy is already upon us. Let us hasten to offer ourselves as a sacrifice to our Father in Heaven. Anyone possessing a knife should slaughter us in sanctification of the One Name of the Everlasting One. Then this person should thrust his sword into either his throat or his stomach, slaughtering himself." They all arose, man and woman alike, and slew one another. The young maidens, the brides and the bridegrooms looked out through the windows and cried out in a great voice: "Look and behold, O Lord, what we are doing to sanctify Thy Great Name, in order not to exchange Your Divinity for a crucified scion who was despised, abominated, and held in contempt in his own generation, a bastard son conceived by a menstruating and wanton woman."[51] They were all slaughtered, and the blood of the slaughter streamed into the chambers where the children of the Sacred Covenant had taken refuge. They lay in rows, babes and aged men together, gurgling in their throats in the manner of slaughtered sheep.

"Wilt Thou restrain Thyself for these things, O Lord?" Avenge the spilt blood of Your servants! Let one and all behold—has the like of this ever occurred? For they all vied with one another, each with his fellow, saying: "I shall be the first to sanctify the Name of the Supreme King of Kings." The saintly women threw their money outside in order to delay the enemy, until they had slaughtered their children. The hands of compassionate women strangled their children in order to do the will of their Master, and they turned the faces of their tender, lifeless children toward the Gentiles.

When the enemy came into the chambers, they smashed the doors and found the Jews writhing and rolling in blood; and the enemy took their money, stripped them naked, and slew those still alive, leaving neither a vestige nor a remnant. Thus they did in all the chambers where children of the Sacred Covenant were to be found.

But one room remained which was somewhat difficult to break into, and the enemy fought over it till nightfall.

When the saints saw that the enemy was prevailing over them, they rose up, men and women alike, and slaughtered the children, and then slaughtered one another. Some of them fell upon their swords and perished, and others were slaughtered with their own swords or knives. The righteous women hurled stones from the windows on the enemy, and the enemy threw rocks back at them. The women were struck by the stones, and their bodies and faces were completely bruised and cut. They taunted and reviled the errant ones with the name of the crucified, despicable, and abominable son of harlotry, saying: "In whom do you place your trust? In a putrid corpse!" The misled ones then approached to smash the door.

There was a distinguished young woman there named Mistress Rachel, daughter of Isaac, son of Asher, who said to her friend: "Four children have I. Have no mercy on them either, lest those uncircumcised ones come and seize them alive and raise them in their ways of error. In my children, too, shall you sanctify the Holy Name of God." One of her friends came and took the knife. When Rachel saw the knife, she cried loudly and bitterly and smote her face, crying and saying: "Where is Your grace, O Lord?" She [the friend] then took Rachel's little son Isaac, who was a delightful boy, and slaughtered him. She [Rachel] had spread her sleeves between the two brothers and said to her friend: "Upon your life do not slaughter Isaac before Aaron."[52] The lad Aaron, upon seeing that his brother had been slaughtered, cried: "Mother, mother, do not slaughter me," and fled, hiding under a box. Rachel then took her two daughters, Bella and Madrona, and sacrificed them to the Lord, God of Hosts, Who commanded us not to depart from His pure doctrine, and to remain wholehearted with Him.

When this pious woman had completed sacrificing three of her children to our Creator, she raised her voice and called to her son Aaron: "Aaron, where are you? I will not spare you either, or have mercy on you." She drew him out by his feet from under the box where he had hidden, and slaughtered him before the Exalted and Lofty God. Rachel then placed them in her two sleeves, two children on one side and two on the other, beside her stomach, and they quivered beside her until finally the errant ones captured the chamber and found her sitting and lamenting over them. They said to her: "Show us the money you have in your sleeves"; but when they saw the slaughtered children, they smote and killed her upon them.

It is of her that it was said: "The mother was dashed in pieces with her children."[53] She perished with them, as did that righteous woman who perished with her seven sons,[54] and it is of her that it was said: "The mother of the children rejoices."[55]

The errant ones slew all those who were inside and stripped them naked as they still quivered and writhed in their blood. "See, O Lord, and behold, how abject I am become."[56] Then they threw them out of the rooms, through the windows, naked, creating mounds upon mounds, heaps upon heaps, until they appeared as a high mountain. Many of the children of the Sacred Covenant were still alive when they were thus thrown, and they gestured with their fingers: "Give us water to drink." When the errant ones saw this, they asked: "Is it your desire to defile yourselves?" The victims shook their heads in refusal and gazed upward to their Father in Heaven, thus saying no, and pointed with their fingers to the Blessed Holy One, whereupon the errant ones slew them.

Such were the deeds of those that have been cited by name. As for the rest of the community, how much more did they do to attest the Oneness of the Holy Name, and all of them fell into the hand of the Lord.

The errant ones then began to rage tumultuously[57] in the name of the crucified one. They raised their banner and proceeded to the remainder of the community, in the courtyard of the count's fortress.[58] They besieged them, too, and warred against them until they had taken the gatehouse of the courtyard and slew some of them as well. A man was there, named Moses, son of Ḥelbo. He called his two sons and said to them: "My sons, Ḥelbo and Simon, at this hour Gehenna is open and the Garden of Eden is open.[59] Which of the two do you desire to enter?" They replied, saying: "Lead us into the Garden of Eden." They extended their throats, and the enemy smote them, father and sons together.

There was also a Torah Scroll in the room; the errant ones

came into the room, found it, and tore it to shreds. When the holy and pure women, daughters of kings, saw that the Torah had been torn, they called in a loud voice to their husbands: "Look, see, the Holy Torah—it is being torn by the enemy!" And they all said, men and women together: "Alas, the Holy Torah, the perfection of beauty, the delight of our eyes, to which we used to bow in the synagogue, kissing and honoring it! How has it now fallen into the hands of the impure uncircumcised ones?"

When the men heard the words of these pious women, they were moved with zeal for the Lord, our God, and for His holy and precious Torah. One young man, by the name of David, son of our Master Rabbi Menahem, said to them: "My brothers, rend your garments[60] for the honor of the Torah!" They then rent their garments in accordance with the instructions of our Sages.

They found an errant one in one of the rooms, and all of them, men and women, threw stones at him till he fell dead. When the burghers and the errant ones saw that he had died, they fought against them. They went up on the roof of the house in which the children of the Covenant were; they shattered the roof, shot arrows at them, and pierced them with spears.

There was a man [there] by the name of Jacob, son of Sullam, who was not of distinguished lineage and whose mother was not of Jewish origin. He called out in a loud voice to all those that stood about him: "All my life, until now, you have scorned me, but now I shall slaughter myself." He then slaughtered himself in the name of Him Who is called Mighty of Mighties.[61] Whose Name is Lord of Hosts.

Another man was there, Samuel the Elder, son of Mordecai. He, too, sanctified the Name. He took his knife and plunged it into his stomach, spilling his innards onto the ground. He called to all those standing about him and declared: "Behold, my brothers, what I shall do for the sanctification of the Eternally Living One." Thus did the elder perish, attesting the Oneness of God's Name and in sanctification of God-fear.

The errant ones and the burghers now departed from there and entered the city, and they came to a certain courtyard where David, the *Gabbai*, son of Nathaniel, was hiding together with his wife, children, and his entire household—the courtyard of a certain priest. The priest said to him: "Behold, not a vestige or remnant has survived in the bishop's courtyard or the count's. They have all been slain, cast away, and trampled underfoot in the streets—except for the few who were profaned. Do as they did, so that you may be saved—you, your money, and your entire household—from the errant ones.

The God-fearing man replied: "Go to the errant ones and to the burghers[62] and tell them all to come to me." When the priest heard the words of Master David, the *Gabbai*, he rejoiced greatly, for he thought: "Such a distinguished Jew has consented to give heed to our words." He ran to them and related the words of the righteous man. They, too, rejoiced greatly and gathered about the house by the thousands and myriads. When the righteous man saw them, he placed his trust in his Creator and called out to them, saying: "Alas, you are children of whoredom, believing as you do in one born of whoredom. As for me—I believe in the Eternally Living God Who dwells in the lofty heavens. In Him have I trusted to this day and in Him will I trust until my soul departs. If you slay me, my soul will abide in the Garden of Eden—in the light of life. You, however, descend to the deep pit, to eternal obloquy, condemned together with your deity—the son of promiscuity, the crucified one!"

Upon hearing the words of the pious man, they flew into a rage. They raised their banners and encamped around the house and began to cry out and shout in the name of the crucified one. They advanced toward him and slew him, his pious wife, his sons, his son-in-law, and his entire household and kin—all of them were slain there in sanctification of the Name. There the righteous man fell, together with the members of his household.

Then they turned and came to the house of Samuel, son of Naaman; he, too, sanctified the Holy Name. They gathered around his house, for he alone of the entire community had remained at home. They asked him to allow himself to be defiled with their putrid and profane water. He placed his trust in his Creator, he and all those with him, and they did not give heed to them [the Crusaders]. The enemy slew them all and cast them out through the windows.

Those who have been cited by name performed these acts.[63] As to the rest of the community and their leaders—I have no knowledge to what extent they attested the Oneness of the Name of the King of Kings, the Holy One, blessed be He and blessed be His Name, like Rabbi Akiba and his companions.[64] May the Lord rescue us from this exile.

The End of the Old Persecutions

Sefer Zekhirah,
or
The Book of Remembrance,
of Rabbi Ephraim
# of Bonn

INTRODUCTION

Like *The Chronicle of Eliezer bar Nathan*, the *Sefer Zekhirah* has enjoyed a certain popularity, possibly attributable to Ephraim's renown as a liturgist of great ability. Four copies of Ephraim's chronicle are known, appearing in the same manuscripts as the four of Bar Nathan's chronicle; these were described in the introduction to Bar Nathan's chronicle.

Born in 1133, Rabbi Ephraim, it seems, was still alive after 1196. Primarily a liturgist in the tradition of the early *pytanim* (composers of *piyyutim* or liturgical poems), he is remembered for a number of legal responsa. In addition, he is the sole source of several prayers based upon earlier Rabbinic traditions, which later entered the standard Ashkenazic liturgy. Ephraim served as the head of the Rabbinic Court at Bonn for some time.

At the time of the Second Crusade, Ephraim was thirteen years old, and, because of his declared presence at the fortress of Wolkenburg during the Crusade,[1] he may be considered, to some extent, an eyewitness of the events described. For this reason his chronicle carries a special authority and is considered an important record of the events involving the Franco-German Jews during the Second Crusade.

The *Sefer Zekhirah* is noteworthy, too, for the beauty of its poetry, reflecting the spirit of Ephraim's *piyyutim*. Of his

117

twenty-five surviving liturgical poems, almost all express his grief at
the suffering endured by the Jews during his lifetime and his hope
for ultimate salvation.

The dating of the *Sefer Zekhirah* is inconclusive. Although the
account itself mentions as living Rabbi Jacob Tam of Rameru, we
cannot assume that the chronicle was composed before 1171, the
year of his death. An earlier passage in the text, which notes the
sainthood of Bernard of Clairvaux ("All the Gentiles regarded this
priest as one of their saints"), if taken literally, places the text after
1174. The ambiguity of such references and their contradictory
nature render any internally based determination of date rather
difficult.

From the point of view of historical accuracy, Rabbi Ephraim's
accounts generally substantiate the reports of parallel, non-Jewish
chroniclers. For example, the whole incident of Radulf's investi-
gations and his subsequent recall by Bernard is readily seen through
several of the latter's *Epistolae*.[2] His report of the events in Würzburg (late February 1147)—including the mention of the discovery
of a Christian corpse, of miraculous ability, said to have been killed
by the Jews—is borne out in sources cited by Aronius.[3] This accusation marks an early development in the evolution of the blood
libel, begun in 1144 with the affair of William of Norwich (or
possibly even as early as the First Crusade[4]) and culminating in the
Black Plague of the fourteenth century.

Ephraim's account of the defeat of the Crusaders at the hands
of the Moslems, particularly his awareness of the number of casualties, is substantiated by general historical sources.[5] His juxtaposition
of an eclipse with the account of the final downfall of the German
Crusaders (undoubtedly a reference to the Battle of Dorylaeum) was
not mere imagination; his dating both of the battle and of the coinci-
dent European eclipse is remarkably accurate.[6]

On the whole, Ephraim's inaccuracies are relatively minor. Evidently through a copyist's error, the events at Cologne are dated
1145, not the accepted 1146. The departure of Conrad III for the
Crusade actually occurred in late May 1147, about six months after
he had yielded to Bernard's plea to take up the Cross—not, as

Ephraim would have it, at the time of the persecutions of the preceding year (spring-fall 1146).

Ephraim's report of Louis VII's cancellation of Crusader debts to the Jews is extreme; in reality, he granted remission from interest and deferred principal payments; never were the debts themselves canceled.[7] This distortion is not characteristic of the *Sefer Zekhirah*. Ephraim in general reveals an eagerness to praise the Christians who were helpful to the Jews. He refers to King Stephen of England, who protected his Jews during the Second Crusade, and does not hesitate to mention a priest, whose identity is unknown to us, who aided the Jews in their time of need.

Interspersed throughout the tales of suffering and persecution is a vibrant liturgical refrain. The author does not, like Solomon bar Simson, merely refer to bits of liturgy; he writes entire sections of lamentation in a manner similar to those appearing in Bar Nathan's chronicle—each commemorating the martyrs of an individual community (Bacharach, Würzburg, Ham, and Sully). Ephraim's language is highly metaphorical, with references to fables, most notably that of the fox and the wolf.[8] Because of his turn of the metaphor and the heavy moral overlay of the liturgy, the characters at times assume powerful, almost mythic, proportions.

As did his contemporaries, Ephraim, too, saw supernatural meaning in natural phenomena. Eclipses, for example, bore fatalistic implications for the writers of both ancient and medieval Jewish literature, as well as for the writers of Christian literature. Like the chroniclers of the First Crusade, Ephraim wished to confirm his belief that the Christians' defeat was punishment for their transgressions against the Jews; thus he associated their defeat with the advent of a red-colored eclipse, which in ancient Jewish lore portended bloody war among the Gentiles. Nevertheless, true solace was found solely through the hope of future redemption in the advent of the Messiah.

Frontispiece of a manuscript of the *Sefer Zekhirah* of Ephraim of Bonn, dating from 1631 and copied from an earlier text. (Courtesy of Bibliothèque Nationale et Universitaire, Strasbourg, France.)

Sefer Zekhirah,
or
The Book of Remembrance,[1]
of Rabbi Ephraim
# of Bonn

*H*earken to me, and I shall recount the matter of the
decree:

I shall write[2] a book of remembrance, relating the incidents of the
    decree,
Regarding the evil and adversity which occurred to the remnant who
    survived
The first bitter decree.
"Blessed be the Lord," we declare,
For having kept us alive to recount these events. In His mercy may
    He speedily avenge us
Upon those who have shed and profaned our blood. And may He
    rebuild the Temple in the city of Zion.

Let this be recorded for later generations to praise and magnify
Almighty God.[3] For Satan came to Ashdod[4] to pillage Israel and
Judah; the enemy traveled in large groups and camped in Haradah.[5]
This occurred in the year 4906 [1146], when our adversaries came
and oppressed Israel. For Radulf was wicked and he treacherously
persecuted the Jews.[6] Radulf, the priest of idolatry, arose against
the nation of God to destroy, slay, and annihilate them just as
wicked Haman had attempted to do. He set forth from France and
traveled across the entire land of Germany—may God spare the
Jewish community there, Amen!—to seek out and to contaminate
the Christians with the horizontal-vertical sign. He went along

121

barking and was named "barker,"[7] summoning all in the name of
Christ to go to Jerusalem to war against Ishmael. Wherever he went,
he spoke evil of the Jews of the land and incited the snake and the
dogs against us,[8] saying: "Avenge the crucified one upon his enemies
who stand before you; then go to war against the Ishmaelites."

Upon hearing this, our hearts melted and our spirit failed us,
because of the fury of the oppressor who intended to destroy us. We
cried out to our God, saying: "Alas, Lord, God, not even fifty
years,[9] the number of years of a jubilee, have passed since our blood
was shed in witness to the Oneness of Your Revered Name on the
day of the great slaughter. Will You forsake us eternally, O Lord?
Will You extend Your anger to all generations? Do not permit this
suffering to recur."

The Lord heard our outcry, and He turned to us and had mercy
upon us. In His great mercy and grace, He sent a decent priest, one
honored and respected by all the clergy in France, named Abbé
Bernard of Clairvaux,[10] to deal with this evil person. Bernard, too,
spoke raucously, as is their manner; and this is what he said to them:
"It is good that you go against the Ishmaelites. But whosoever
touches a Jew to take his life, is like one who harms Jesus himself.
My disciple Radulf, who has spoken about annihilating the Jews, has
spoken in error, for in the Book of Psalms it is written of them:
'Slay them not, lest my people forget.'"[11]

All the Gentiles regarded this priest as one of their saints,[12] and
we have not inquired whether he was receiving payment for speaking
on behalf of Israel. When our enemies heard his words, many of
them ceased plotting to kill us. We also gave our wealth as ransom
for our lives. The Lord, being merciful to us, permitted a remnant to
survive on the earth and enabled us to remain alive. Whatever they
asked of us, either silver or gold, we did not withhold from them.[13]
Were it not for the mercy of our Creator in sending the aforementioned Abbé and his later epistles,[14] no remnant or vestige would
have remained of Israel. Blessed the Redeemer and Savior, blessed
be His Name!

In the month of Elul,[15] at the time when Radulf the priest—
may God hound and smite him—arrived at Cologne, Simon the
Pious, of the city of Trier, returned from England where he had

spent some time.[16] When Simon came to Cologne, he boarded the vessel to return to Trier. As he set out from Cologne to board the ship, he encountered worthless persons who had been defiled by the abominable profanation. They entreated him to profane himself [i.e., to become baptized] and deny the Living God. He refused, remaining steadfast in loving and cleaving to his God. Then came persons of brazen face who severed his head from his body by placing it in a winepress and then cast away his pure corpse.

When the Jews of the city heard of this, they grieved, their hearts went out, and they became fearful, and they said: "Behold the days of reckoning have come, the end has arrived, the plague has begun, our days are completed, for our end is here. We declare: 'We have been cut off!'"[17] The people wept exceedingly for the precious soul that had perished and been cut off from the land of the living because of the transgressions of my people. The leaders of the community went and spoke to the burghers requesting the return of the saint's head and body. After receiving a bribe, the burghers returned the corpse, and the righteous man was brought to Jewish burial. May his soul rest in goodness, and his seed inherit the earth.

A Jewish woman named Mistress Mina of Speyer left the city, and they seized her and cut off her ears and the thumbs of her hands; thus did she suffer for the sanctification of her Creator. Happy is the people whose lot is thus; happy is the people whose God is the Lord.

At that time Judah and Israel declined to the lowest level, and the day of retribution drew near. The children of Israel lifted up their eyes and saw the despicable errant oppressors advancing from every direction and pursuing them to slay them. They were greatly frightened and lifted up their eyes to the mountains and the fortresses.[18] Each one besought a Gentile acquaintance, anyone who owned either castle or fortress, to receive shelter from him—that is, to allow him to enter the crevices of the rocks and hide there until the wrath had passed.

After the feast of Tabernacles in the year 4906,[19] they departed from the cities and made their way to the fortresses. The majority of the community of Cologne gave a large sum to the bishop of Cologne[20] so that he would give them the fortress of Wolkenburg.[21] This was the securest refuge in Lorraine.[22] They gave the nobleman, keeper of the fort, many gifts, so that he would leave the fort and hand it over to them alone, and no stranger or uncircumcised one was allowed to join them.[23] They all pledged their lives and their homes and wealth in the city of Cologne to the bishop as collateral.

From the time the Gentiles were informed that Wolkenburg had been given to the Jews and that they were gathering there, they ceased pursuing them, and thus relief came for all the rest of the Jews who were fleeing to the castles.[24]

I, the young author of this narrative, was thirteen years old when I dwelled with my kinsmen in the fortress of Wolkenburg. Most of them were related to my mother, may her soul rest in Eden. The other Jews of all the king's provinces gathered together and arose in defense of their lives. They saved themselves and their families by seeking refuge in the fortresses of Gentile acquaintances.

When we first arrived at Wolkenburg, there was an old Jew living in the village at the foot of the mountain who had two handsome sons named Abraham and Samuel. In their youthful inpetuousness, they decided to ascend the mountain to us, to see what we were about. A wicked man, a brazen Gentile who neither respected the aged nor had compassion for youth,[25] met them, struck and slew them, and went his way. Some youngsters coming down the mountain saw the bodies of the boys lying dead, and they went and told the father of the murdered boys. Their father wept for them, and he mourned his sons many days. Later it became known who had murdered them, and the community paid the bishop a bribe, and he ordered that the culprit be seized. They gouged out the eyes of the murderer, and three days after he was blinded, the villain's heart ceased and he turned to stone. Thus the Lord struck him down, and he died and turned into a putrid corpse. May all Thine enemies perish thus, O Lord. And the two youths were brought to Cologne for burial and were interred there. May their souls rest in the Garden of Eden.

Two Jews from Mainz, Isaac, son of Joel, the Levite, and Master Judah, were making wine at the time of the grape harvest. A despicable oppressor marked with a horizontal line against a vertical one [i.e., a cross] ambushed them and slew them; then he went off to everlasting abhorrence[26] and never returned. A nobleman came to [their] house and confiscated all of their possessions.[27] The slain Jews were brought to Mainz, where they were buried in their family plots.

There was a Jew of Worms, a valorous and pleasant man, Samuel, son of Isaac. At that time, some oppressors attacked him on the road between Mainz and Worms and slew him. But he succeeded in wounding three of the enemy. His community had his body brought back to his city, and he was buried there.

Three Jews, together with their families, escaped to the Stahleck fort: Alexandri, son of Moses, an accomplished student; Abraham, son of Samuel; and Kalonymos, son of Mordecai. They had formerly lived in the village of Bacharach at the foot of that mountain. On that day, on the eve of Pentecost, it was decreed by the King[28] that they should descend the mountain to look into their debts and other matters. The errant ones rose up against them and pursued them, demanding that they defile themselves. They refused, for they deeply loved their Creator even unto death.[29] Kalonymos openly spat on the image of the crucified one, and they slew him on the spot. The others took refuge under beds, but were slashed and pierced by the swords of the enemy. All of them were buried in Mainz. At that time there was no king to protect Israel from the errant ones, who would take up Israel's cause, for King Conrad had himself donned the abominable sign and set out for Jersusalem;[30] and Judah and Ephraim cried out:

O heavens, all the nations bear their impurity upon the fringes of
    their garments;
They sin in promiscuity and violence,
Yet they are secure and live in expansive circumstances.[31]
I, however, have endured doubly
From the Lord's hand, because of His great wrath;
I have drained the goblet and its remnant.

In the year 4907 [1147], my blood, too, was drawn from me and caused to decay. Hear, O Lord, for we have been shamed!

I wail on the day of turmoil, and sob 'midst muted wails
For the murdered ones of Bachrach on whom God's wrath was
    vented,

A tombstone of a Jewish woman, one of the early victims of the
Second Crusade. The fragmented inscription reads: ". . . . daughter
of Isaac, [who was murdered] and drowned in Sanctification of the
Oneness of God, in the year 906 [1146] on the Friday, the fifth of
Iyar [19 April]. May she rest in Eden, the Garden." See *Jahrbuch
der Vereinigung "Freunde der Universität Mainz"* 8 (1959): 71–72.
(Courtesy of Professor Eugen Ludwig Rapp, Mainz.)

126

Causing the blood of the pious to be shed. And because of our sins
    the slaughter persists.
Oppressed by the sword and the drawn bow, their soul and spirits
    downcast,
They were pursued relentlessly by the enemy, being granted no rest.
May their memory be blessed,
And may the right hand of God sustain them, giving them refuge
    beneath the Tree of Life.

Other Jews, too, were seized and forcibly defiled with the
disgusting water. They escaped, however, and were saved, and that
very night they fled and returned to their Lord, the Holy One of
Israel. A Jewish woman by the name of Gutalda, of blessed memory,
was seized at Aschaffenburg,[32] but she refused to be profaned with
the bitter, accursed water.[33] She santified the Holy Name and
drowned herself in the river. May God remember her for good, as He
recalls the Matriarchs Rachel and Leah.

On the twenty-second day of the month of Adar,[34] the evildoers
attacked the community of Würzburg,[35] for the other communities
had already fled to the rocks and fortresses. The inhabitants of
Würzburg had anticipated living in tranquility, but instead they
endured distress and destruction. The enemy made false accusations
in order to justify their attack upon them. They declared: "We have
found a Gentile in the river whom you slew[36] and threw there. He
has thus achieved sainthood and is working miracles."

As a result, the errant ones and the poorer segment of the population, those who derive joy from things of no consequence, arose
and smote the Jews. A saintly person named Rabbi Isaac, son of our
Rabbi Eliakim, a modest and humble man, venerable and pleasant,
was slain over his book; and there were twenty-one others with him.
One of them was a Hebrew lad, an accomplished student, by the
name of Simon, son of Isaac, who suffered twenty wounds and then
survived for fully a year. They took his sister to their place of
idolatry so as to profane her, but she sanctified the Name and spat
upon the abomination. They then struck her with stone and fist, for
they do not bring swords into the disgusting house. She did not die,
but lay prostrate upon the ground feigning death. They bruised,
struck, and burnt her repeatedly to determine whether or not she
had truly died. They then placed her on a marble slab, but she did
not awaken or make the slightest motion with her hand or foot.

Thus did she deceive them till nightfall. Finally a Gentile laundress came and bore her to her home, where she concealed her and saved her life. The remaining Jews took refuge in the courtyard of their neighbors. On the following day, they fled to Fort Stuhlbach. Blessed is He Who granted them rescue.

Alas, my melancholy soul yearns as does the hart,
For the slain of Würzburg, a community like a vine intertwined.[37]
How is it suddenly slaughtered, and sunken to the lowest level?
Therefore I weep in sorrow, my spirit and soul are melted,
I shall not grant myself respite. She that was adorned with the commandments as with a wreath,[38]
How is she now set forth naked, and has drawn back in shame!
Henceforth their portion in life shall be to abide in the Garden of Eden, arrayed in a circle,
Standing there in a ring, transcending temporal life,[39]
In eternal existence, constant ascent, abounding in strength and exultation.

On the following day, the bishop[40] ordered that all the slaughtered saints be collected on wagons—all the choice severed limbs: hips and shoulders, thumbs of hands and feet, sanctified with holy oil, together with everything else that remained of their bodies and limbs—and buried in his garden. Hezekiah, son of our Master Rabbi Eliakim, and Mistress Judith, his wife, purchased this Garden of Eden[41] from the bishop and consecrated it as an eternal burial ground. "May the generous one be blessed for his bountifulness, for having given."[42]

Also in Ham,[43] about one hundred and fifty people were slain. May God remember them for good.

My heart cries out in anguish for the slain of Ham: their saints have been given over to slaughter!
Their great multitude! How have its ranks been diminished,
And the plunderer has beset them! Therefore shall I eulogize them!
For their heroes are fallen and they are devoid of speech.
How dear to me was their friendship, for they abounded with good deeds,

Like the fullness of pomegranates and their sections.[44] Their share
   is with the righteous;
None may enter into their realm.[45] How great is their merit!
For they have bound their sacrifices and prepared their offerings,
Like Isaac, their father.
May their virtue stand as merit for their children,
That God have mercy on them in the land of their servitude, and
   prolong their days in peace.

In Sully,[46] too, a great many people were slain:

My heart is lifeless within me; "Woe and Alas" do I wail
For the slain of Sully. Weeping, I sound my voice in lament,
Like the shrill cry of first birth and illness, for the slaughter of my
   offspring.
Alas, God, my Creator, how many will be led to slaughter?
To the dust of the path trampled under the wayfarer[47] did he
   liken me; gall and wormwood has he fed me;
With the slime of the road has he engulfed me; slaying my suckling
   and child.
Lord, God, my Strength—declare the bestowal of beneficence upon
   me![48]
For You are my God, to Whom I gave my blood at the time of
   circumcision;
And I cast away my life to declare Thy Oneness. You heal all my
   ailments!
Make an end to my mourning, and establish me wholly upon a
   firm foundation,
O Lord, my Rock and my Redeemer!

In Carentan,[49] too, countless people were slain; for they had
gathered together in one courtyard, and the enemy came upon them
suddenly. There were two young men, valiant brothers, who stood in
defense of their own lives and those of their brethren. They slew and
wounded their enemies, and the foe could not prevail against them,
until the enemy came upon them from the rear into the courtyard
and slew all of them.

Rabbi Peter,[50] the Great Rabbi, disciple of our Master Rabbi
Samuel and his brother, our Master Rabbi Jacob of Rameru,[51] was

slain as he marched in the funeral procession of a deceased *Parnass.*
Woe to the generation that has lost so precious a pearl! To whom is
it lost, if not to its owner? Woe to the ship that has lost its cap-
tain![52] Woe to the eyes that have beheld his fall! Woe to the heart
that remembers his slaying. Come, brethren and friends, and mourn
your master who clothed you in scarlet and in other elegant raiment.
O, Daughters of Israel, weep exceedingly, like jackals and
ostriches.[53] Call out:

O my brother, my spirit is bitter, I am distraught in my complaint!
O Master, Whose glory has been dimmed. Alas, the tongue that is
    eloquent in speech,
Joyous as a gazelle in subtle Talmudic disputation, speaking erudite
    utterances—
Why has it licked the dust and been cut off from the Book?
The lofty cluster of henna, how has it been cut,
Thus muting the tongue of the sage and the scribe![54] God Who
    forgives and reprieves,
Whose counsel no man can annul—
Accept him as ransom for his people.

On the second festival day of Pentecost, the errant ones from
the land of France gathered at Rameru, and they came to the house
of our Master Rabbi Jacob, may he live,[55] and took all that was in
his house. They ripped up a Torah Scroll before his face and took
him out to a field. There they argued with him about his religion and
started assaulting him viciously. They inflicted five wounds upon his
head, saying: "You are the leader of the Jews. So we shall take
vengeance upon you for the crucified one and wound you the way
you inflicted five wounds on our god."[56]

His pure soul would have perished were it not for the mercy of
our Creator, Who had mercy upon him on account of the merit of
his Torah study. The Lord caused an eminent nobleman to pass
through the field in which our Master Rabbi Jacob was to be found.
Our master called to him and offered him a bribe of a horse worth
five *zekukim.*[57] The nobleman went and spoke to the errant ones
and persuaded them, saying: "Leave him be for today and I will
speak to him. Perhaps he will be tempted and we shall succeed in
swaying him. Should he refuse, know that I will hand him back to

you tomorrow." They consented, and the evil hour was thereby averted.

Thus God in His compassion for His people had mercy upon him who propagates His Holy Torah amongst them. As for the other French communities, we have not heard of any person being slain or forcibly converted at that time, but they did lose much of their wealth, for the king of France[58] had proclaimed: "Whosoever volunteers to go to Jerusalem will receive remission of any debt he owes to the Jews."[59] Most of the loans of the Jews in France were on trust, and so they lost their money.

In England, the Most High King rescued them through the instrument of the king of England,[60] putting it into his heart to protect them and save their lives and property. Blessed be He Who aids Israel.

Those who had been forcibly converted in the various communities returned to the true path in that same year [4] 907 [1147]. Blessed be He Who grants strength, for He provided a priest who guided them to the land of France and other lands, so that they might return to their Torah and remain in those places until their defilement had worn off and been forgotten. For this he took neither silver nor gold. Blessed be He Who performs miracles for all who trust in Him and draw near to Him.

On the fifteenth of Av[61] in the year [4] 907, all the communities had already returned to their native lands and dwelt in their cities and in their homes as before. The errant ones had already passed through and were headed toward Topheth and Gehenna.[62] Blessed be the God Who wreaks vengeance, for most of them never returned to their homes, nor did their communities ever see them again. Some of them died of starvation, some by the plague or sword, and some from the exhaustion of the sea crossing. Furthermore, the hand of the Lord was upon any evildoer who had laid a hand upon a Jew. Only a small number[63] of the murderers—not even one out of a hundred—ever returned to their homeland.

On the New Moon of Kislev,[64] in the year [4] 908, there was an eclipse of the sun when a third of the day had passed; inside the eclipse could be seen the shape of a wagon wheel. It had a number of hues: red, green, and black.[65] This scene lasted for an hour, and then the sun reverted to its normal appearance. Afterwards we learned that on that day the Christians had warred with the Ishmaelites and that the Christians had fallen. And in the course of their entire journey they conquered only one little town called Lascona,[66] on the border of the Land of Israel. They expelled the native population and dwell there to this day. They did the same to Ashkelon, which belonged to the Philistines. Some say that Ashkelon was subsequently retaken by the Philistines.[67]

May the jealous and vengeful God reveal to us His vengeance against both Edom and Ishmael, as He did against Pharaoh and all of Egypt; as the fox declared in song to the animals after the repast.[68]

May the blood of our pious ones that was spilt like water seethe His purple garment,[69] as His son Rabbi Meir declared: "When a man is pained, what does the Divine Presence say? 'My head is heavy upon me, my arm is heavy upon me.' And if God suffers such anguish for the spilt blood of the wicked,[70] how much more is His mercy aroused for the spilt blood of the righteous?" For Israel has been compared to the dove, as it is written: "Thine eyes are [as] doves."[71] Whereas all other birds struggle and quiver upon being slaughtered, and the dove does not, but rather stretches out its neck, so do none except Israel offer their lives for the Blessed Holy One, as it is written: "For Thy sake are we killed all the day, etc."[72]

And the Holy Torah which they tore and trampled will cry out in anguish and protest before its Creator, and He will topple them and cast them down into the dust.

The reward of pious persons who were slain bearing witness to the Oneness of the Name is homiletically expounded in the Midrash *Lekah Tov* and *Shohar Tov*[73] on the passage "How Great is Your Goodness!"[74] to the effect that each martyr possesses eight vestments, like a High Priest, and two crowns. Moreover, their glory surpasses that of the High Priest, for the High Priest sprinkled the blood of sacrifices, whereas they sprinkled their own blood and the blood of their precious children; they bound '*Akedot*, erected altars, and prepared sacrifices. May God remember them to the good, and may their righteousness stand the entire congregation of Israel in good stead forever and ever.

May the Rock Who is white and ruddy[75] overturn Edom as He
    did Sodom.
"So that my glory may sing praise to Thee, and not be silent."[76]
And may He inflict upon the accursed nation of Ishmael the
    upheaval of Gomorrah.
May He lead back the stray lamb as in former times, to its abode,
May He erect the chosen Edifice in splendor and in majesty,
And make the crown resplendent as before. Restore unto us com-
    plete Sovereignty
Over the entire domain once entrusted unto us. And give over the
    entire Land [of Israel] into our hands.
As of yet, we suffer great privation, for, while copper may be
    replaced with gold,[77]
What recompense can be made for Rabbi Akiba and his colleagues?
    But no! We cannot question the ways
Of Him Who is fearful and awesome. We must always declare His
    righteousness.
It is we who have sinned; what can we then say?[78] May His
    strength be aroused
And his mercies awakened upon us, amen. May it thus speedily
Occur upon the completion of the Book of Remembrance.

      Completed is the Book of Remembrance, annal of events.
         Blessed be the Rock of Perfection,
           The Lord abounding in mercy.
And may I, Ephraim the youth, be amongst those who shall be granted
      The full measure of solace assured in the Torah.
             Amen, amen.

Notes/Index

Notes

GENERAL INTRODUCTION

1 See S. Runciman's introduction to *A History of the Crusades*, 3 vols. (London: Penguin, 1965), 1:xi. Also relevant are H. E. Mayer, *The Crusades* (Oxford: Oxford University Press, 1972), pp. 1-179, and his *Bibliographie zur Geschichte der Kreuzzüge* (Hanover: Hahnsche Buchhandlung, 1960; second unaltered edition, 1965), supplemented by the same author in "Literaturbericht über die Geschichte der Kreuzzüge," *Historische Zeitschrift*, 3 (1969): 641-731. Of special importance is K. M. Setton, gen. ed., *A History of the Crusades*, vol. 1: *The First Hundred Years*, ed. M. W. Baldwin (Madison: University of Wisconsin Press, 1969), chaps. 7, 8, 15. For additional data and bibliography, see the selected bibliographies culled by J. A. Brundage in *The Crusades: A Documentary Survey* (Milwaukee: Marquette University Press, 1962) and *Medieval Canon Law and the Crusader* (Madison: University of Wisconsin Press, 1969). For Jewish sources and material, see S. W. Baron, *A Social and Religious History of the Jews* (New York: Columbia University Press, 1957), vol. 4, chap. 21, and B. Z. Dinur, *Yisrael ba-Golah* [Israel in the Diaspora] (Jerusalem: Mosad Bialik, 1965), 2 (bk. 1): 1-89. Also see J. Prawer, *Toldot mamlekhet ha-Ẓalbanim be-'Ereṣ Yisrael* [A history of the Latin kingdom of Jerusalem], 3d ed., 2 vols. (Jerusalem: Mosad Bialik, 1971), 1:3-66, 71-113, regarding the First Crusade, and pp. 251-99, regarding the Second Crusade. Although Prawer's book is mainly a thorough history of the Crusaders' kingdom in the Holy Land, it offers a lucid account of the events in Europe and in the Jewish communities affected by the Crusades, in addition to a comprehensive bibliography.

2 The Crusader assault upon the Jewish community of Rouen is known to us through non-Jewish sources only. See Guibert of Nogent, *De vita sua, Recueil des historiens des Gaules et de la France*, ed. M. Bouquet et al., 24 vols. in fol. (Paris, 1738-1904), 12:240. Of the actual letters of warning sent by the French communities to the Rhineland, our information is

derived solely through the anonymous chronicle. See *Mainz Anonymous*, p. 99.

3 See Cosmas of Prague, *Chronicon*, 3. 4, in *Monumenta Germaniae Historica, Scriptores*, ed. G. H. Pertz, T. Mommsen et al. (Hanover: Reichsinstitut für ältere deutsche Geschichtskunde, 1826-), 7:103 (hereafter cited as *MGH, SS*). Also see S. Steinherz, "Kreuzfahrer und Juden in Prag 1097," *Jahrbuch der Gesellschaft für Geschichte der Juden in der Cechoslovakischen Republik*, 1 (1929): 16-18, and *Germania Judaica*, vol. 1: *From the Earliest Times to 1238*, ed. I. Elbogen, A. Freimann, and H. Tykocinski (Tübingen: J. C. B. Mohr, 1963), pp. 508-12.

4 See *Bar Simson*, n. 44.

5 See Runciman, *History of the Crusades*, 1:134-35, and Mayer, *The Crusades*, pp. 42-44.

6 See his *Epistolae ad Ludovicum Regem*, in *Patrologiae Cursus Completus: Patrologia Latina*, ed. J. P. Migne, 221 vols. (Paris: 1844-55), vol. 189, cols. 366 ff.

7 Concerning the history of the Second Crusade and the concurrent persecution of the Jewish communities, see V. G. Berry, "The Second Crusade," in Setton, *History of the Crusades*, 1:463-89. For additional information conerning Bernard of Clairvaux and his role in restraining anti-Jewish excesses during the Crusade, see *Sefer Zekhirah*, nn. 10, 11, 14.

8 See A. M. Habermann, *Toldot ha-piyyut ve ha-shirah* [A history of Hebrew liturgical and secular poetry], 2 vols. (Ramat Gan: Massada, 1972), 2:167-214, and A. Mirsky, "Makhẓevatan shel ẓurot ha-piyyut" [The origins of forms of liturgical poetry], in *Studies of the Research Institute of Hebrew Poetry in Jerusalem* 7 (1958): 3-10.

9 See P. Alphandéry, "Les citations bibliques chez les historiens de la première croisade," *Revue d'histoire des religions* 99 (1929):139-57.

10 See H. Bresslau's critical introduction to A. Neubauer and M. Stern's *Hebräische Berichte über die Judenverfolgungen während der Kreuzzüge* (Berlin: Leonhard Simion, 1892), pp. xxiii-xxiv.

11 Note Porges' article, "Les rélations hébraïques des persécutions des juifs pendant la première croisade," *Revue des études*

juives 25 (1892): 181–201; 26 (1893): 183–97 (hereafter cited as *REJ*).

12 See I. Elbogen's "Zu den hebräischen Berichten über die Judenverfolgungen im Jahre 1096," in *Festschrift zum siebzigsten Geburtsage Martin Philippsons* (Leipzig: Gustav Fock, 1916), pp. 6–24.

13 This contention is advanced by I. Sonne in "Nouvel examen des trois rélations hébraïques sur les persecutions de 1096, suivi d'un fragment de version judéo-allemande inédite de la première relation," *REJ* 96 (1933): 113–56, and in his Hebrew article, "'Ezehu ha-sippur ha-kadum 'al gezerot TaTNU" [Which is the earlier account of the persecutions during the First Crusades?], *Zion* 12, nos. 1–2 (1946–47): 74–81. I. F. Baer, in "Gezerot TaTNU" [Persecutions of 1096] in *Sefer Assaf*, ed. M. D. Cassuto, J. Klausner, and J. Gutmann (Jerusalem: Mosad ha-Rav Kook, 1953), pp. 126–27, leaves the problem of historical sequence unresolved. As for textual differences, he asserts that originally there existed various independent accounts, which were combined into coherent wholes by three different compilers; discrepancies in the texts are to be ascribed to errors of transcription. Though such errors may exist in particular details, the narratives as a whole are reliable and cohesive. Also see S. Eidelberg, "The Solomon bar Simson Chronicle as a Source of the History of the First Crusade," *Jewish Quarterly Review* 49 (1959): 282–87.

14 Regarding organized self-defense efforts, see *Bar Simson*, pp. 30, 46, 68, and cf. *Mainz Anonymous*, p. 104. The Czech account may be found in the *Rýmovaná Kronika Česka* [Czech rhymed chronicle] of Dalimil in *Fontes rerum bohemicarum* 3:182; the relevant portions are translated and discussed by Steinherz, "Kreuzfahrer und Juden," pp. 1, 18–22.

In 1288, in the wake of a ritual-murder libel in the Rhineland involving a youth named Wernher, we find mention of five hundred Jews present at a sermon of exoneration, unwillingly delivered by the archbishop of Mainz, who threatened death to any dissenting congregant. See *Chronicon Colmariense*, in *MGH, SS.*, 17:255. Most likely, however, the reference to Jews is not literal, but refers here to impious Christians, as J. Parkes suggests (*The Jew in the Medieval*

Community [London: Soncino, 1938], p. 128, n. 1), to the imperial troops sent by King Rudolph in response to a Jewish bribe.

15 From other, more explicit medieval sources, we may conclude that certain Jews were permitted to bear arms for the purpose of self-defense. See the privilege granted by Bishop Rüdiger of Speyer in 1084, which required the Jews to participate in the internal defense of the city (J. Aronius, *Regesten zur Geschichte der Juden in Fränkischen und Deutschen Reiche* [Berlin: Leonhard Simion, 1902], No. 358a). In addition, see the responsum of R. Isaac ben Moses of Vienna (*'Or Zaru'a*) of the early thirteenth century, in which he condemns certain Bohemian Jews for carrying their swords and shields on the Sabbath, in violation of B. *'Eruvin* 45a. In the *Responsa of Rabbi Meir of Rothenburg* (Prague ed., 1608, Nos. 576, 978), certain responsa, in dealing with collaterals of arms owned by Jews, may to some extent imply Jewish possession of arms.

16 See *Bar Nathan*, p. 82; *Mainz Anonymous*, p. 104; and *Sefer Zekhirah*, p. 129.

17 See Ezekiel, chaps. 38, 39. In Talmudic lore, the war of Gog and Magog will precede the coming of the Messiah, as in, e.g., B. *Sanhedrin* 97b.

18 See Genesis 22: 1-20. On the *'Akedah* as a symbol of martyrdom in Christian literature, see H. L. Strack and P. Billerbeck, *Kommentar zum Neuen Testament*, 3 vols (Munich: C. H. Beck, 1924), 2:225-26.

19 See A. H. Silver, *A History of Messianic Speculation in Israel* (New York: Macmillan, 1927), pp. 58-80, and G. Scholem, *The Messianic Idea in Judaism and other Essays on Jewish Spirituality* (New York: Schocken, 1972), pp. 1-26. Scholem here maintains that the bitter experiences of the German Jews during the Crusades served to turn them to the study of mysticism. Even as late as the seventeenth century, Nathan Schapiro, a Polish mystic, regarded 1096 as a speculative date for the initiation of the Messianic era; that the Messiah had not appeared was due to the sins of the Jews. See G. Scholem, "Ha-Tenu'a ha-Shabbetai'it be-Folin" [Sabbatianism in Poland] in *Beit Yisrael be-Folin*, ed. I. Halperin, 2 vols. (Jerusalem: Zionist Organization, 1954), 2:40.

20 See H. Chadwick, *The Early Church* (London: Penguin, 1969), pp. 29-30, 123, 271.

21 The prayer *'Av ha-Raḥamim* [May the Father of Mercies] was probably composed soon after the First Crusade in 1096. Ephraim of Bonn notes that as early as his time (during the Second Crusade) this prayer was recited. Its recital originally followed the reading of a list of martyrs. Today the prayer is included only in the Ashkenazi Rite, and, in certain liturgies, is recited only on the Sabbath before the Fast of Av, commemorating the Destruction of Jerusalem as well as the martyrs of the Crusade. See E. E. Urbach, ed., *Sefer 'Arugat ha-Bosem* of R. Abraham bar Azriel (Jerusalem: Mekiẓe Nirdamim, 1963), 4:49, n. 51.

THE CHRONICLE OF SOLOMON BAR SIMSON: INTRODUCTION

1 See I. Sonne, "Le-bikoret ha-tekst shel ha-sippur 'al gezerat TaTNU le R. Shlomo bar Simson" [Critical annotation to Solomon bar Simson's record of the First Crusade], in *The Abraham Weiss Jubilee Volume* (New York: Yeshiva University Press, 1964), p. 385.

2 Guibert of Nogent, *Historia Hierosolymitana*, 2.8, in *Recueil des historiens des croisades*, 16 vols. in fol. (Paris: Académie des inscriptions et belles-lettres, 1841-1906), *Historiens Occidentaux*, 5 vols. (1841-1895), 4:142-43 (hereafter cited as *RHC, Occ.*).

3 See Albert of Aix, *Liber Christianae expeditionis pro ereptione, emundatione, et restitutione sanctae Hierosolymitanae ecclesiae*, 1.7, in *RHC, Occ.*, 4:276.

4 Ekkehard of Aura, *Hierosolymita*, in *RHC, Occ.*, 5(pt. a):21; Albert of Aix, *Liber Christianae expeditionis*, 1.23-24, in *RHC, Occ.*, 4:289-91.

5 Albert of Aix, *Liber Christianae expeditionis*, 1.7, in *RHC, Occ.*, 4:276.

6 Ibid., 1.9, in *RHC, Occ.*, 4:278; and cf. K. M. Setton, gen. ed., *A History of the Crusades*, vol. 1: *The First Hundred Years*, ed. M. W. Baldwin (Madison: University of Wisconsin Press, 1969), pp. 260-61.

7 See *Bar Simson*, n. 195.

8 Ibid., n. 6.

9 Possibly Wesseli—see ibid., n. 216.

10 Oxford: Oxford University Press, 1886, No. 28, p. 11.

THE CHRONICLE OF SOLOMON BAR SIMSON

1 The opening passage is obscure. I. Sonne, "Le-bikoret ha-tekst
   shel ha-sippur 'al gezerat TaTNU le R. Shlomo bar Simson"
   [Critical annotation to Solomon bar Simson's record of the
   First Crusade], in *The Abraham Weiss Jubilee Volume* (New
   York: Yeshiva University Press, 1964), p. 385, suggests that
   Bar Simson's account was preceded by a register of martyrs of
   the three prominent Rhine communities of Speyer, Worms,
   and Mainz. See also A. Neubauer and M. Stern, *Hebräische
   Berichte über die Judenverfolgungen während der Kreuzzüge*
   (Berlin: Leonhard Simion, 1892), p. 81, n. 1.
       However, when one examines the frontispiece of the sole
   manuscript of this chronicle, a disparity in handwriting is
   readily apparent. It would seem that this opening section was
   tacked on by a copyist at a later date.

2 The medieval rabbinical tradition dated the destruction of the
   Temple to the year 68 C.E. rather than 70 C.E. (1028 + 68 =
   1096).

3 The letters of the Hebrew word for "sing," *Ranu*, are numer-
   ically equivalent to 256. The embolic cycle of nineteen lunar
   years, seven of which have thirteen months each, had been
   adopted by the Jews in order to adjust the solar calendar to
   their lunar calendar. The end of the 255th cycle of nineteen
   years was 4,845 = 1085 C.E. The addition of eleven years of
   the 256th cycle thus yielded the year 1096 C.E. The 256th
   embolic cycle thus suggested hope for salvation during this
   period of nineteen years and clearly reflected the messianic
   expectations of the era. See A. H. Silver, *A History of Messianic Speculation in Israel* (New York: Macmillan, 1927), p.
   58, and G. Scholem, *The Messianic Idea in Judaism and other
   Essays on Jewish Spirituality* (New York: Schocken, 1972),
   pp. 1–36.

4 Jeremiah 31:7.

5 In text, *tokhahot*, or "admonitions." The Hebrew term alludes
   to the section in Leviticus 26:14–45 and the parallel section in
   Deuteronomy 28:15–69.

6 The fact that women and children accompanied the Crusaders
   is also known through non-Jewish sources. See, e.g., Albert of
   Aix, *Liber Christianae expeditionis pro ereptione, emenda-
   tione, et restitutione sanctae Hierosolymitanae ecclesiae*, 1.7,

in *Recueil des historiens des croisades*, 16 vols. in fol. (Paris: Académie des inscriptions et belles-lettres, 1841-1906), *Historiens Occidentaux*, 5 vols. (1841-1895), 4:272 (hereafter cited as *RHC, Occ.*). J. Mann, "Ha-tenuot ha-meshihiot bime masa'e ha-zelav ha-rishonim" [Messianic movements during the days of the earlier Crusades], *Ha-Tekufah* 23 (1925): 253, and D. Kaufmann, "A Hitherto Unknown Messianic Movement among the Jews," *Jewish Quarterly Review*, o.s. 10 (1898): 139. This passage is an example of the narrator's knowledge of the historical development of the Crusade, which is exhibited throughout the narrative.

7 Proverbs 30:27. The Christian chroniclers of the Crusades made similar use of Biblical metaphors in reference to the Crusaders and their acts; e.g., the myriads of Crusaders were compared to locusts. See Guibert of Nogent, *Historia Hierosolymitana*, 1.1, *RHC, Occ.*, 4:125, and I. F. Baer, "Gezerot TaTNU" [Persecutions of 1096], in *Sefer Assaf*, ed. M. D. Cassuto, J. Klausner, and J. Gutman (Jerusalem: Mosad ha-Rav Kook, 1953), p. 128.

8 In text, *beit ha-tarput*, or "house of idolatry," after B. *'Avodah Zarah* 29b. Evidently the chronicler infused his own religious bias into his account of the Christians' speech.

9 The chronicler seems to have been aware of the causes which inspired the zealousness of the Crusaders. The parallel with the argument reported by Guibert of Nogent in *De vita sua*, 2.5, in *Recueil des historiens des Gaules et de la France*, ed. M. Bouquet et al., 24 vols. in fol. (Paris, 1738-1904), 12:240, is readily apparent. An interesting syntactical parallel is easily drawn with the text of a Geniza letter of Obadyah (Johannes), a Norman convert of the eleventh century. A. Scheiber in his article "Ein aus arabischer Gefangenschaft befreiter christlicher Proselyt in Jerusalem" (*Hebrew Union College Annual* 39 [1968]: 163-75) published the fragmented text of the letter. The linguistic parallels with the Crusaders' declaration at the opening of our chronicle are outstanding and raise several questions about the origins of the chronicles. Did Obadyah see an early prototype of the Jewish chronicle, or perhaps both he and our chronicler drew from a common Gentile pamphlet circulating at the time of the Crusade? As the information relevant to this point is limited, no definitive answer can be given at this time. See S. D. Goitein's illumi-

nating article, "Obadyah, a Norman Proselyte" in *The Journal of Jewish Studies* 4 (1953): 80–81, and cf. N. Golb, "Persecution at the Time of the First Crusade," *Proceedings of the American Academy for Jewish Research* 34 (1966): 31–32.

10 Our narrator's derogatory references to the Holy Family were influenced by an earlier work known as *Ma'aseh Yeshu*, and also as *Toldot Yeshu*. See S. Krauss, *Das Leben Jesu* (Berlin: S. Calvary and Co., 1902), pp. 41, 204, 288. Cf. J. Rosenthal, "Sifrut ha-vikuah shel yeme ha-beynayim" [Rebuttal and attack in the Jewish polemical literature of the Middle Ages], *Proceedings of the Fifth World Congress of Jewish Studies* 2 (1969): 356–58. See also *Bar Simson*, introduction.

11 Meaning the religious practices of their ancestors during perilous times, namely: prayer, charity, and repentance. See J. *Ta'anit* 2:1 and Midrash *Genesis Rabba*, 44:15.

12 Exodus 32:34.

13 Psalms 103:20.

14 In text, [*rosh*] *hodesh*, referring to the day on which the coming month would begin. Iyar is the eighth month of the Hebrew calendar, varying between April and May.

15 The names of the eleven martyrs of Speyer were compiled by E. Carmoly in *Ben Hananja Wochenblatt für jüdische Theologie*, No. 5 (3 February 1864): 91–92. Cf. S. Salfeld, *Das Martyrologium des Nürnberger Memorbuches* (Berlin: Leonhard Simion, 1898), p. 101.

16 The reference is to Bishop John of Speyer (1090–1104). See J. Aronius, *Regesten zur Geschichte der Juden in Fränkischen und Deutschen Reiche* (Berlin: Leonhard Simion, 1902), No. 183, and A. Hauck, *Kirchengeschichte Deutschlands* (Leipzig: Hinrich Verlag, 1906), 3:990.

17 An ambiguous reference perhaps alluding to a fuller description given in a parent vesion (see general introduction), preserved only in the *Mainz Anonymous* and only alluded to weakly here in the *Bar Simson*.

18 The name of the bishop of Worms of this period was Adalbert or Allenbrand (Aronius, *Regesten*, No. 184). However, Schiffmann is uncertain as to whether Bishop Adalbert still served in Worms in the year 1096. See S. Schiffmann, *Heinrich IV und die Bischöfe in ihrem Verhalten zu den deutschen Juden zur Zeit des ersten Kreuzzüges* (Berlin: Friedrich-Wilhelm University, 1931), p. 28.

19 The month of Sivan is the ninth month of the Hebrew calendar, varying between the months of May and June.

20 Hosea 10:14.

21 Lamentations 4:5.

22 This is an allusion to the register of martyrs which preceded Bar Simson's account. See above, n. 1.

23 Ezekiel 38:4; 39:9. In the text the phrase "shield and protection" is *magen ve-zina*, a play on the place-name Magenza, one of the early medieval names of Mainz.

24 It seems that Emicho ignored the order of Emperor Henry and attacked Speyer on 3 May 1096. The same troops assaulted the Jews in Worms on 18 May. A second attack on the Worms community by a local mob occurred on 25 May. See Aronius, *Regesten*, Nos. 183, 184, and 185.

25 Cf. Judges 6:13. In alluding to the verse, the narrator substituted Edom for Midian. "Edom" is a general term referring to any non-Jewish tyranny or oppression, particularly Christian; see J. Rosenthal, *Meḥkarim u-Mekorot* [Studies and sources] 2 vols. (Jerusalem: R. Mass, 1967), 1:280.

26 Referring to Archbishop Ruthard of Mainz (1089–1109). See Aronius, *Regesten*, Nos. 185, 187, and G. Meyer von Knonau, *Jahrbucher des Deutschen Reiches unter Heinrich IV und Heinrich V*, 7 vols. (Leipzig: Dunker and Humblot, 1890–1909), 5 (1892): 252.

27 A metaphor borrowed from Ecclesiastes 9:12.

28 A Talmudic saying. See B. *Baba-Bathra* 138a.

29 On the desire of the archbishops of the Rhine communities to protect the Jews against the Crusaders, see Schiffmann, *Heinrich IV und die Bischöfe*, pp. 28–41. Her contention is based mainly on the premise that the attitudes of the bishops were molded in strict accordance with the political situation of the times—the conflict between Henry IV and the Papacy over lay investiture. Regarding the trend of economic competition between Jews and Christians at this time, see W. Roscher, "Die Stellung der Juden im Mittelalter, betrachtet vom Standpunkte der allgemeinen Handelspolitik," *Zeitschrift für die gesamte Staatswissenschaft* 31 (1875): 503–26.

30 On Godfrey of Bouillon and his leading role in the Crusade, see Knonau, *Jahrbücher* 4 (1890): 259, and S. Runciman, *A History of the Crusades*, 3 vols. (London: Penguin, 1965), 1: 145–46.

31 A Midrashic expression referring to the enemies of Israel. See
    Midrash *Genesis Rabba*, chap. 49.

32 After Isaiah 58:12, referring to the saintly pious as repairing
    the iniquitous breach created by their contemporaries.

33 Talmudic allusion to the act of martyrdom. See B. *Menaḥot*
    110a.

34 On Rabbi Kalonymos, son of Rabbi Meshullam, see L. Zunz,
    Gottesdienstlichen Vorträge der Juden historisch entwickelt
    (Berlin: A. Asher, 1832), pp. 378, 403; and *Germania Judaica*,
    vol. 1: *From the Earliest Times to 1238*, ed. I. Elbogen, A.
    Freimann, and H. Tykocinski (Tübingen: J. C. B. Mohr, 1963),
    p. 196. The aura of greatness surrounding the personage of
    Rabbi Kalonymos bar Meshullam can be traced chiefly to the
    Bar Simson chronicle and to a lesser extent to the *Mainz
    Anonymous*—in no other medieval Jewish source is he men-
    tioned except in the legend concerning his part in the publi-
    cation of the liturgical poem *U-Netaneh Tokef*, chanted on the
    High Holy Days. The oldest mention of this legend is found in
    the *'Or Zaru'a* of Rabbi Isaac ben Moses of Vienna (Žitomir
    ed., 1862), vol. 2, No. 276, in the name of Ephraim of Bonn.
    See S. Eidelberg, "Ha-Reka ha-histori shel ma'aseh R. Amnon
    u-tefilat u-Nataneh Tokef" [The historical background of the
    legend of Rabbi Amnon and the *u-Netaneh Tokef* prayer],
    Hadoar 3 (1974): 645–46.

35 The official leader of the community—an office generally
    reserved for men of unquestionable character and piety. See
    B. *Yoma* 22b, and cf. *Jewish Encyclopedia*, 9:541.

36 Although we have no record of a privilege awarded to the Jews
    of Mainz, possibly Rabbi Kalonymos was defending a privilege
    given earlier of which no record exists. See Schiffmann,
    Heinrich IV und die Bischöfe, p. 27.

37 Our narrator was in error concerning two points. First, the
    reference to Apulia is incorrect, for the emperor then resided
    in northern Italy and not in the Apulia region to the southeast.
    (An Italian variation of Apulia, Paglia, is employed in two
    Hebrew chronicles of a later period. See *Josippon* [Mantua ed.,
    1480], at the end of the narrative, and also B. Klar, ed.,
    Megillat 'Aḥima'aṣ [The chronicle of 'Aḥima'aṣ] [Jerusalem:
    Tarshish, 1944], pp. 20, 24, 38, 55). Second, Emperor Henry
    IV spent seven years in Italy (1090–1097), and not nine years
    as stated by the narrator. See Aronius, *Regesten*, Nos. 170,
    171, 178, 183.

38 On Henry IV's order to Godfrey not to molest the Jews on the Crusade, see E. Täubler, "Urkundliche Beiträge zur Geschichte der Juden in Deutschland im Mittelalter," in *Mitteilungen des Gesamtarchivs der Deutschen Juden*, 5 (1915): 143–44, but, as mentioned above, Godfrey did not fulfill his oath to Henry.

39 Godfrey of Bouillon received a large bribe in Cologne. One *zakuk*, according to an early medieval source, was worth twelve ounces of silver. Thus five hundred *zekukim*, the amount paid to Godfrey, was the equivalent of six thousand ounces—a sizeable sum. See S. Eidelberg, *The Responsa of Rabbenu Gershom Me'or ha-Golah* (Hebrew) (New York: Yeshiva University Press, 1955), p. 94. However, a later source equates a *zakuk* with eight ounces of silver; see L. Zunz, *Zur Geschichte und Literatur* (Berlin: Veit and Co., 1845), p. 543. See *Mainz Anonymous*, n. 41.

40 Psalms 124:5. On the "evil waters" as referring to baptism, see E. E. Urbach, "Études sur la littérature polémique au moyen-age," *Revue des études juives* 100 (1935): 55.

41 Cf. Acts of the Apostles 5:30. In text, *talui* means he who was hanged or crucified. In the chronicles it is used as a reference to Jesus.

42 Cf. Matthew 27:25.

43 See, e.g., John, chap. 8. At this point the chronicler mentions a known Christian contention that God abandoned the Jewish people and chose the Christians for his children. See, e.g., E. E. Urbach, ed., *Sefer 'Arugat ha-Bosem* of R. Abraham bar Azriel (Jerusalem: Mekiẓe Nirdamim, 1963), 4:47; *Sefer Niẓahon* (Vetus) (Altdorf: J. C. Wagenseil, 1681), pp. 253–56; and Menahem ben Aaron ibn Zeraḥ, *Ẓeidah la-Derekh* (Warsaw: N. H. Herzog, 1880), p. 40. A similar Christian contention is recorded even as late as the seventeenth century in the *Ma'aseh Tuvia* [Deeds of Tuvia] (Venice, 1708) of the physician Tuvia Katz (b. 1652). See A. Levenson, *Tuvia ha-Rofeh* [Tuvia the physician] (Berlin: Rimon, 1924), p. 25.

44 This is a reference to the speech of Pope Urban II at Clermont on 27 November 1095. See D. C. Munro, "The Speech of Pope Urban II at Clermont," *American Historical Review* 11 (1906): 231–42.

Although our narrator regards the Council of Clermont as the cause of the Crusade which in turn engendered the persecution of the Jews, a later thirteenth-century Jewish legend relates the cause of the Jewish persecution to a hoax perpetrated by two priestly pilgrims said to have been insulted by Jews on a visit to the Holy Sepulchre. In revenge they placed an anonymous note on the tomb of Jesus beseeching all Christendom at the command of Jesus to destroy the Jews and all disbelievers in his word.

The legend continues that this note was brought before "the gathering of nations," a reference to the Council of Clermont. Immediately, the tale claims, all those gathered there swore to fulfill the command delineated in the note and attack the Jewish communities en route to the Holy Land. See Urbach, introduction to *'Arugat ha-Bosem*, 4:183-84. Urbach maintains there that this legend is basically an adaptation of a Christian legend concerning Peter the Hermit's role in the causes of the First Crusade. See Albert of Aix, *Liber Christianae expeditionis*, 1.2-5, *RHC, Occ.*, 4:272-73.

45 A reference to the Christians. See Genesis 36:20; Isaiah 24:4.

46 Isaiah 40:15. The prophet's expression "a drop of the bucket" has a disparaging meaning.

47 Psalms 78:60; also see, in B. *Megillah* 29a, the interpretation of the verse "Yet have I been to them as a little sanctuary in the countries where they are come (Ezekiel 11:16)" as referring to all synagogues after the destruction of the Temple. Hence the meaning of the text is: God forsook the "miniature temple," or synagogue, which had been His home amongst His people. (Cf. Exodus 25:8.)

48 A goose said to be possessed of magical powers and serving as a guide and a mascot for Crusaders is similarly mentioned by Albert of Aix, *Liber Christianae expeditionis*, 1.25, in *RHC, Occ.*, 4:291.

49 A reference to the quorum of ten adult male Jews required for congregational prayer.

50 Regarding the tale of the souls praying in the synagogue at night, see *Sefer Ḥasidim* [The book of the pious] (Frankfurt a.M., 1924), No. 711, and cf. S. Eidelberg, "The Solomon bar Simson Chronicle as a Source of the History of the First Crusade," *Jewish Quarterly Review* 49 (1959): 284, n. 20.

51 Ezekiel 11:13.

52 Psalms 119:137.

53 Emicho, count of Leiningen, commanded a band of Crusaders. Regarding his acts of depredation in the Rhineland, see also Albert of Aix, *Liber Christianae expeditionis*, 1. 27, *RHC, Occ.*, 4:292.

54 On Emicho's claim to have a cross miraculously branded to his flesh, see Runciman, *A History of the Crusades*, 1:137. Peter the Hermit had an illusion similar to Emicho's.

55 In text, "Italy of Greece," which refers to the ancient Greek seaport colonies in southern Italy.

56 Archbishop Ruthard of Mainz. Ruthard's role in the events of Mainz is partly recorded in the Latin sources. See Schiffmann, *Heinrich IV und die Bischöfe*, p. 33, and above, n. 29.

57 The text is ambiguous. From the account in the *Mainz Anonymous*, we may conclude that the precise rendition is *mamonenu*, "our money," not *memunenu*, "our emissary," as rendered by A. M. Habermann, *Sefer Gezerot Ashkenaz ve-Zorfat* [The persecutions of France and Germany] (Jerusalem: Tarshish, 1945; reprint edition, Ofir, 1971), p. 29. The purpose of the letter was to instruct the Jewish communities en route to provide Emicho and his group with money and provisions. See p. 62, where a similar instance is mentioned regarding a letter brought by Peter the Hermit from the French Jews requesting their German brethren to provide him with food and money.

58 In accordance with Genesis 18:20-33.

59 Corresponding to 27 May 1096. For a detailed summary of the events in Mainz, see Aronius, *Regesten*, No. 185.

60 Exodus 19:15.

61 2 Samuel 1:23.

62 See above, n. 32.

63 Lamentations 1:6.

64 Isaiah 28:6, referring to wars of justice.

65 See *Sayings of the Fathers* 1:1. The implication here is that the Jews of Mainz were so scrupulous in the practice of their religion as to adhere to certain precautionary prohibitions in addition to the prescribed statutes.

66 Obviously Emicho and the burghers betrayed the Jews of Mainz and opened the gate for the Crusaders. See also Eidelberg, "The Solomon bar Simson Chronicle," pp. 283-84.

67 On the Jews' right to bear arms, see G. Kisch, *The Jews in Medieval Germany* (Chicago: University of Chicago Press, 1949), p. 111; Eidelberg, "The Solomon bar Simson Chronicle," p. 284, n. 18; Eidelberg, "Hukim germaniim be-'ahat ha-teshuvot shel RaGMa" [German jurisprudence in a responsum of Rabbenu Gershom], *Zion* 18, nos. 1-2 (1953): 83-87; and general introduction, pp. 11-13, and n. 15.

68 The text in the manuscript is ambiguous. It seems that, deceived by a ruse by Emicho, who had it rumored that he was leaving the city, the Jews weakened their defense. See Eidelberg, "The Solomon bar Simson Chronicle," p. 284.

69 In text, *to'evah*, "abomination," a term frequently employed by the Hebrew chroniclers to indicate the Church. See Proverbs 28:9.

70 For a discussion of the four Talmudic methods of capital punishment (stoning, burning, beheading, strangulation), see B. *Sanhedrin* 50a.

71 This is based on the account of R. Akiba's martyrdom mentioned in B. *Berakhot* 61b.

72 A reference to a Talmudic scholar of keen ability. See, e.g., B. *Berakhot* 64a, and B. *Sanhedrin* 24a.

73 See above, n. 10.

74 *Sayings of the Fathers* 5:4.

75 See Daniel 1:6-19.

76 In text, *akdu*, "they bound," an allusion to the *'Akedah*, or the traditional binding of Isaac. See S. Spiegel, *The Last Trial* (Philadelphia: Jewish Publication Society, 1967), pp. 3-8.

77 Isaiah 33:7. The association of this verse with Isaac is found in Midrash *Genesis Rabba* 56:6.

78 My translation of this verse employs the rendition of the Hebrew *sar* as "sun," deriving from the root *zhr*, or "light." See D. Yelin, *Hikre Mikra* [Biblical studies] (Jerusalem: Darom Books, 1929), p. 7, on Isaiah 5:30. It must be realized however that *sar* might indeed refer to an adjective meaning "dismal," in which case the verse would read slightly differently. In addition, the chronicler may have altered the Biblical *ba'arifeha*, referring to the clouds, substituting *be'arifatam*, referring, by the use of a homonym, to the beheading of the slain Jews. Cf. *Bar Nathan*, p. 83.

79 Rabbi Eliezer bar Nathan reports that 1,300 were killed in Mainz. See *Bar Nathan*, p. 83, and n. 20.

80 Lamentations 2:1.

81 Judaism values highly all anonymously given charity. Cf. Proverbs 21:14 and, in Maimonides' *Mishneh Torah, Hilkhot Matnot 'Aniyim* [Laws of charity] 10:8.

82 Lamentations 2:5.

83 Cf. Isaiah 17:6.

84 Deuteronomy 6:4.

85 *The Narrative of the Old Persecutions*, or *Mainz Anonymous*,

records the name as Rabbi Menaḥem, the son of Rabbi David ha-Levi. See also *Germania Judaica*, p. 192.

86 In text, *Shekhinah*, a term referring to the Divine Countenance. In this context: Divine inspiration departed from Jacob and he was suddenly unable to foresee the future. Therefore, instead of continuing with "that which shall befall you in the end of days," he turned to the immediate concern of his sons.

87 See the Madrashic elucidation of Genesis 49:1-2 in the *Targum* of Jonathan Ben Uziel ad loc. and B. *Pesaḥim* 56a, according to which Jacob conjectured that his forefather Abraham was imperfect for he fathered Ishmael—and Isaac, too, for he fathered Esau. Therefore, Jacob wondered what defect he had which caused his power of prophecy to be impeded. His sons replied in unison, "Hear, O Israel, etc.," thus indicating that they all submitted themselves unquestioningly to the yoke of heavenly judgment. Similarly Menaḥem addresses himself to his fellow Jews, saying that they, too, must faithfully accept God's verdict.

88 Exodus 24:7.

89 The Jews' fear of losing their children to Christendom is a recurring motif in Hebrew literature, even appearing in the twentieth-century poet S. Tchernichovski. See S. Eidelberg, "Ha-Yesod ha-Histori be-Shirat Tchernichovski" [Historical elements in Tchernichovski's poetry], *Hadoar* 43 (1963): 162-64. See *Mainz Anonymous*, p. 103.

90 In the text, *ma'akhelet*, a term reminiscent of the language of Genesis 22:10, where the story of the *'Akedah* is recounted.

91 A reference to the basin used for the dispersing of blood in the Temple rite. See, e.g., Exodus 29:18-21; Zechariah 14:20.

92 Deuteronomy 18:13.

93 Hosea 10:14.

94 This is a reference to the martyrdom of Hannah and her seven sons at the time of Antiochus Epiphanus, mentioned in 2 Maccabees, chap. 7.

95 Psalms 113:9.

96 Lamentations 1:11.

97 See B. *Mo'ed Katan* 26a, where the rending of one's garment as an act of mourning after witnessing the desecration of a Torah Scroll is prescribed.

98 The actual phrase in the text is *'Adir 'Adirirum*, which is a cabalistic name for the Divine. See G. Scholem, *Major Trends in Jewish Mysticism* (New York: Schocken, 1961), p. 55, and

p. 363, n. 57. See also *Mainz Anonymous*, n. 61.

99 An honorary synagogue official.

100 Compare B. *Gittin* 57a, where this is the prescribed punishment for infidelity.

101 In text, *Shavuot*, or the feast of Pentecost, which falls on the sixth of Sivan.

102 At this point the text is obscured and was emended according to Rabbi Eliezer bar Nathan's version. See p. 84.

103 In other words they were forcibly converted, and therefore it was assumed that they were doomed to Hell.

104 He did so in emulation of the priestly ritual upon the Temple altar. See Leviticus 8:11; 2 Kings 9:33.

105 Psalms 50:23.

106 The practice of converting synagogues into churches in times of persecution and expulsion was common throughout the Middle Ages in Europe. See, e.g., J. Parkes, *The Conflict of the Church and the Synagogue* (Philadelphia: Jewish Publication Society, 1961), pp. 213–14. With respect to Spain, see I. F. Baer, *A History of the Jews in Christian Spain* (Philadelphia: Jewish Publication Society, 1966) 2:96–97, 101.

107 On Rabbi Eleazar, see *Germania Judaica*, p. 448, and A. Aptowitzer, *Introductio ad Sefer Rabiah* (Jerusalem: Mekize Nirdamim, 1939), p. 310.

108 Isaiah 57:1. Cf. the corresponding Talmudic interpretation in B. *Sota* 49b.

109 In accordance with B. *Ketubot* 67b.

110 This refers to the ten leading scholars who were martyred during the second century C.E. by the Romans. For a description of the liturgy on "The Ten Martyrs," see *Jewish Encyclopedia*, 8:355.

111 In B. *Berakhot* 48b, where this passage serves to emphasize the importance of the burial of martyrs.

112 Psalms 110:6.

113 Psalms 94:1.

114 Exodus 19:11.

115 See Aronius, *Regesten*, No. 185, for varying accounts of the toll.

116 Sacristia or Secretarium, a storage room for priestly vestments.

117 Deuteronomy 28:48.

118 Here the narrator concludes the story of the martyrdom of the *Parnass*, Rabbi Kalonymos bar Meshullam, which he began above. See p. 30.

119 On the attitude of the archbishop of Mainz to the Jewish com-

munity and his endeavor to rescue them, see Schiffmann, *Heinrich IV und die Bischöfe*, pp. 32-33.

120 Isaiah 64:11.
121 Psalms 110:6.
122 Deuteronomy 32:43.
123 Psalms 83:13.
124 Psalms 83:5.
125 Psalms 94:7.
126 Psalms 94:1.
127 Psalms 44:23.
128 Isaiah 9:11.
129 Lamentations 2:20-21.
130 Psalms 79:12.
131 Psalms 94:2.
132 Isaiah 13:5.
133 Isaiah 42:13.
134 Psalms 79:6.
135 Psalms 69:25.
136 After Ezekiel 26:4, 14.
137 Psalms 79:10.
138 Cf. Deuteronomy 12:15.
139 Leviticus 22:28.
140 The events at Cologne are described in greater detail in the account of Rabbi Eliezer bar Nathan. See pp. 85 ff.
141 See B. *Ta'anit* 29a, and *Targum* to Ecclesiastes 12:11.
142 The month Tammuz follows Sivan.
143 The communities of Speyer, Worms, and Mainz.
144 On efforts by local Gentiles in Cologne to protect the Jews, see also Schiffmann, *Heinrich IV und die Bischöfe*, pp. 40-41.
145 Ezekiel 7:22.
146 Lamentations 1:11.
147 Namely Archbishop Hermann III of Cologne. See Aronius, *Regesten*, No. 188.
148 A reference to the following villages, throughout which Hermann III, archbishop of Cologne, dispersed the Jews: Neuss, Wevelinghofen, Eller, Xanten, Mehr, Kerpen, and Geldren. See Salfeld, *Martyrologium*, pp. 418-22, and cf. *Germania Judaica*, p. 244 and Arenius, *Regesten*, No. 188.
149 Referring to the feast of St. John, which fell on the twenty-fourth of June.
150 Psalms 68:23, and see B. *Gittin* 57b. The Talmud interprets this verse as assuring resurrection to religious martyrs. See below, n. 209.

151 According to Rabbi Eliezer bar Nathan's report, the name of
     the village was Wevelinghofen, southwest of Neuss. See p. 86.
152 Wevelinghofen was surrounded by marshlands. The chronicler
     used the Hebrew *'agam*, or "pond," to refer to these marshes
     for want of a better word.
153 The chronicler was in error regarding this point. The river that
     passed near Wevelinghofen was not the Rhine but the Erft. Bar
     Nathan omits mention of the Rhine in this context.
154 2 Samuel 1:23.
155 In text, "with *patbag*," king's food, an allusion to food ritually
     unfit to eat. See, e.g., Daniel 1:5; 11:26.
156 Isaiah 64:11.
157 Isaiah 41:13.
158 Deuteronomy 32:43.
159 An allusion to Neuss and Wevelinghofen. See *Bar Nathan*, pp.
     86–87.
160 In text, *'Ilana*, a corruption of Eller. See above, n. 148.
161 Throughout this period the fairs of Cologne served both as
     commercial centers and as communal gathering places for the
     Jews of the Rhine. See C. Brisch, *Geschichte der Juden in Cöln*
     (Mülheim am Rhein: Carl Mayer, 1879), p. 17; A. Kober,
     Cologne (Philadelphia: Jewish Publication Society, 1940), pp.
     11–14; and Eidelberg, *The Responsa of Rebbenu Gershom*,
     p. 94.
162 See Judges 18:1. The narrator does not mean literally that the
     man was from the tribe of Dan. He hints at his strict observ-
     ance of the law by using a play on the Hebrew words *Din*,
     "law" and *Dan*, "the tribe." See Genesis 49:16. Cf.
     Kaufmann's comment in "Hitherto Unknown Messianic Move-
     ment," p. 150, n. 1.
163 Psalms 15:1; see the entire psalm.
164 Corresponding to the year 1140 C.E. See general introduction,
     pp. 10–11, and n. 13; also pp. 15–16 above.
165 Genesis 2:1–3. These verses introduce the blessing over the
     wine (*Kiddush*) in the Sabbath Eve liturgy.
166 "Son of Aaron" is probably a reference to Rabbi Moshe ha-
     Cohen (the priest). In the chronicles the motif of priesthood
     involved also a willingness to submit to self-sacrifice and
     martyrdom. Cf. B. *Sanhedrin* 111a.
167 See Ezekiel 4:3 and the Talmudic exegesis in B. *Berakhot* 32b,
     where the metaphor of the copper griddle appears.

168 Song of Songs 1:3. The author's interpretation is based on a play on the Hebrew word *'alamot*, "maidens," which he reads *'ad mavet*, "unto death." Hence the chronicler implies a willingness on the part of the martyrs to sacrifice their very lives to demonstrate their love for God. The quotation is incorrectly ascribed to King David rather than to King Solomon; compare Midrash *Song of Songs Rabbah* ad loc., and Urbach, *'Arugat ha-Bosem*, 4:49.

169 Psalms 44:23.

170 Rabbi Akiba symbolized in the Talmud the highest degree of martyrdom (see B. *Berakhot* 61b) and became a prototypical figure for the martyr during the religious persecutions of the Middle Ages.

171 Genesis 14:18. A priest is generally accorded the honor of leading the Grace-after-Meals.

172 If the company consists of three or more males at least thirteen years of age, he who leads in saying Grace summons the rest to join him in thanking "Him of Whose bounty we have partaken." This custom is ancient, and the formulae, still in use today, are found in the Mishnah (*Berakhot* 7:3).

173 This prayer deviates from the normal text of Grace. Rabbi Moses is interpolating supplications appropriate to the somber circumstances.

174 Cf. 2 Chronicles 34:12. Meaning those involved in the events of the time. The abrupt return to the first person is perhaps indicative of a common authorship in the narratives of Eller (pp. 53-55) and Xanten.

175 See Numbers 28:1-4, 8.

176 Psalms 19:6.

177 Isaiah 64:3.

178 After Ezekiel 8:17. The reference is to an act of disdain toward the offered baptismal rites.

179 A reference to Jerusalem; see Isaiah 29:1.

180 The day of the month is missing in the text. However, in the account of Rabbi Eliezer bar Nathan (see p. 88), the day is given as the seventh of Tammuz, which fell on 30 June, 1096. Cf. Aronius, *Regesten*, No. 196.

181 Av is the eleventh month of the Jewish calendar, varying between July and August. The ninth of Av is traditionally observed as a fast day, commemorating the destruction of the Temple.

182   In text, *zehuvim*, meaning gold pieces; the specific amount is not mentioned by our narrator; however, Bar Nathan mentions only one gold piece. See p. 89.

183   Tremonia is the Latin name of Dortmund in Westphalia.

184   The person who wrote the account interpolated the words "our erroneous belief" in the statement of the Gentile, to show complete dissociation from Christian dogma even when quoting a statement attributed to Christians. It is possible that this is not necessarily an intentional offense, but rather a mode of expression common at that time. See S. W. Baron, *A Social and Religious History of the Jews* (New York: Columbia University Press, 1957), 4:290.

185   Judges 5:31.

186   In text, *tekufat tammuz*, which generally denotes that quarter corresponding to the months of June–August.

187   Deuteronomy 33:2.

188   Psalms 16:11.

189   See Midrash *Leviticus Rabba*, chap. 30, for this play on the homographic words *sheva*, "seven," and *sova*, "satiety."

190   Psalms 31:20; 5:12; 97:11.

191   On the desecration of Jewish cemeteries in other cities of medieval Germany, see Kisch, *Jews in Medieval Germany*, p. 184.

192   An allusion to Volkmar's massacre of the Jews of Prague, despite the protests of Bishop Cosmas (30 June 1096). See Cosmas of Prague, *Chronicon*, 3. 4, in *Monumenta Germaniae Historica, Scriptores*, ed. G. H. Pertz, T. Mommsen et al. (Hanover: Reichsinstitut für ältere deutsche Geschichtskunde, 1826–), 7:103 (hereafter cited as *MGH, SS.*).

193   As Wesseli is in Bohemia, the final textual reference is ambiguous. Perhaps the copyist confused the last letter of Wesseli (*yod*) with the graphically similar conjunction *vav*, or "and." Thus the meaning is actually "Wesseli in Bohemia" as opposed to the original "Wessel[i] and in Bohemia." See *Germania Judaica*, pp. 510-11, and B. Z. Dinur, *Yisrael ba-Golah* [Israel in the Diaspora] (Jerusalem: Mosad Bialik, 1965), 2 (bk. 1): 32, 52, n. 32.

194   In 1096 C.E.

195   The reports of the events in Trier differ in this chronicle from those in Christian sources. Bar Simson, as usual, notes only a small number of converts to Christianity during the assault upon the Jewish community, including a certain Rabbi Micah.

Nevertheless, these sources report that all Jewish converts returned to Judaism in 1097, save Rabbi Micah. See *Gesta episcoporum Trevirorum*, 17, in *MGH, SS.*, 8:190–91, and Aronius, *Regesten*, Nos. 176, 189.

196 Peter the Hermit (Peter of Amiens). On Peter and his role in the First Crusade, see Runciman, *History of the Crusades*, 1: 113–15, 123–26.

197 See above, n. 57, for a similar affair involving Emicho of Leiningen.

198 In text, "land of Lothair," referring to an area which includes the Rhineland and Lorraine. At the time of the chronicles, the Rhineland was still called Eretz Lothair by the Jews, due to the fact that it had been part of the kingdom of Emperor Lothair I (840–844 C.E.). See *Germania Judaica*, pp. 160–62.

199 Egilbert, archbishop of Trier, 1070–1101. See Aronius, *Regesten*, No. 189.

200 Lamentations 1:9.

201 They ate after nightfall, as is the practice for various minor fasts which commence at sunrise and conclude once night has fallen.

202 Literally, "assembly." See Leviticus 23:36; Numbers 29:35; Deuteronomy 16:8. This term is used in Rabbinic literature to designate the holiday of *Shavu'ot*, or Pentecost, which is celebrated on the sixth of Sivan, six weeks after Passover.

203 The narrator thus concludes the first portion concerning the tragic events of Trier with fragmented verses from the Bible, e.g., Exodus 32:34; Deuteronomy 11:17; Jeremiah 27:22; Ezekiel 39:23.

204 In text, *timon*, a corruption of Simon. This may refer to the Talmudic idiom *timyon*, connoting total oblivion, a derogatory innuendo alluding to the church. See B. *Sukah* 29b, and Midrash *Leviticus Rabba*, chap. 19.

205 Emperor Henry IV was in Italy during the Crusaders' march through Germany. (See above, n. 37.) However, it seems that his imminent return was awaited.

206 After Lamentations 2:16; 3:46, meaning "those who open their mouths to speak evil against us."

207 See above, n. 178.

208 Deuteronomy 28:32.

209 Psalms 68:23. This verse is cited in the Talmud with regard to a similar act of martyrdom on the part of Jewish youths being taken to Rome for immoral purposes. See B. *Gittin* 57b, and

compare a related incident in *Sefer ha-Qabbalah*, ed. and trans.
G. D. Cohen (Philadelphia: Jewish Publication Society, 1967),
p. 64.

210 The massacre at Metz has already been mentioned, see p. 62;
here, however, the account is more detailed. Runciman,
History of the Crusades, 1:139, maintains that Metz was attacked by Emicho's troops who returned to Lorraine after the
massacre of Jews at Trier. However, Aronius (*Regesten*, Nos.
180–81) maintains that the attack on Metz occurred while the
Crusaders were first passing through Lorraine on their way to
Germany. Our narrator, while compiling the events in
Germany, added the account in Lorraine without attaching
any importance to the difference in geographical location. His
motive was to report the great martyrdom of the Jews, without much attention to geographical and chronological details.

211 After Isaiah 23:8, 9.

212 The number twenty-two agrees with the number mentioned in
the *Mainzer Memorbuch*. See Aronius, *Regesten*, No. 181.

213 After Isaiah 26:20.

214 The narrator does not tell us which particular group of Crusaders attacked the Jewish community at Regensburg
(Ratisbon). According to Aronius (*Regesten*, No. 199), the
attack was made by Emicho's group on 23 May 1096. However, Runciman, *History of the Crusades*, 1:140, maintains
that the attack on Regensburg was led by Gottschalk, who
penetrated into Bavaria. Cf. K. M. Setton, gen. ed., *A History
of the Crusades*, vol. 1: *The First Hundred Years*, ed. M. W.
Baldwin (Madison: University of Wisconsin Press, 1969), p.
262.

215 The narrator mentions that the forced converts at Regensburg,
who included most of this Jewish community, returned later
to Judaism. The narrator does not mention the fact that they
returned to Judaism only in 1097, following the return of
Henry IV from Italy. Pope Clement III, however, tried unsuc-
cessfully to countermand Henry's allowance for the Jews'
return. See Aronius, *Regesten*, Nos. 103–4.

216 Such a location is unknown to us, and probably the copyist
erred. For a summary of the hypotheses regarding this place,
see Baron, *Social and Religious History*, 4:103, 291. However,
it seems that B. Z. Dinur's suggestion (*Yisrael ba-Golah*, 2 [bk.
1]:35, 52) is the most acceptable. He suggests that Šla is
Wesseli in Bohemia, a community on the road between

Regensburg and Prague. See above, n. 193.

217 "Land of Ḥori"—Genesis 36:20–21. Cf. Isaiah 34:12. Ḥori may refer to Austria. Cf. L. Zunz, *Die synagogale Poesie des Mittelalters* (Frankfurt a.M.: Kaufmann Verlag, 1920), p. 438.

218 Referring to Peter the Hermit (also known as Peter of Amiens).

219 King Coloman I of Hungary.

220 After Numbers 21:21–22.

221 Denarius, an ancient Roman coin. The narrator uses this term for a coin of unknown denomination in use at this time.

222 Through comparison with the course of events reported in Christian sources, this location can most probably be identified with Semlin. See *Bar Simson*, introduction.

223 *Ma'ah* is a small denomination. See M. Jastrow, *Dictionary of Talmud Babli, Yerushalmi, Midrashic Literature, and Targumum* (New York: Pardes, 1950), 2:813. It is used here in reference to a small coin whose value is unknown to us.

224 Stoning is the prescribed punishment for idolatry in Jewish law. See B. *Sanhedrin* 49b–50a. Our chronicler had Peter accuse the Hungarians of idolatry in terms meaningful to his Jewish audience, namely the applicable Talmudic law.

225 See *Bar Simson*, introduction, p. 18.

226 In text, Innsbruck. However, this is not acceptable since its location is not near the known route followed by the Crusaders. The reference may be to a city known then as Wieselburg, which was located in western Hungary not far from the Austrian border, near the present-day Magyaróvar. Wieselburg, also known as Moson on the Leitha, is recorded in Hungarian sources as the place in which the Crusaders were bogged down. See I. Katona, *Historia Critica Regum Hungariae*, 42 vols. (Pestini: Weingrad and Koepf, 1779–1817), vol. 3, chap. 19, and cf. Runciman, *History of the Crusades*, 1:140.

227 In text, *Yevanim*, or "Greeks." The chronicler refers to the Bulgarians, who, as Byzantine subjects, were often referred to as Greeks in medieval literature. See S. Eidelberg, "Sefer Bi'ur 'al ha-Torah" [A commentary on the Pentateuch], *Horeb* 14–15 (April 1960): 246–48.

228 Regarding the excessive number of Crusaders killed by the Hungarians as estimated in the chronicle, see Eidelberg, "The Solomon bar Simson Chronicle," p. 287, n. 35. It is possible that our chronicler attributed to the Hungarian campaign the

casualties sustained by the Crusaders throughout the entire First Crusade.

229 Emicho and several German knights managed to escape and return to their homes, bringing back accounts of their venture. Such reports evidently reached the Jews. Like the Jews, some Christians saw in Emicho's defeat a punishment for murdering the Jews. See Albert of Aix, *Liber Christianae expeditionis,* 1.29, in *RHC, Occ.,* 4:295; and Ekkehard of Aura, *Hierosolymita,* in *RHC, Occ.,* 5 (pt. 1):21.

230 The appearance of an eclipse was taken to be an evil omen throughout the Middle Ages. The chronicler's dating of the eclipse "at that time" is highly ambiguous. It may refer to an eclipse which occurred on 20 August 1096, about the time of Emicho's defeat on the banks of the Danube at Wieselburg. However, it may also refer to a later eclipse over southeastern Europe, on 25 December 1098. See T. R. von Oppolzer, *Canon of Eclipses,* trans. Owen Gingerich (New York: Dover, 1962), p. 220, and chart 110 at end. See *Sefer Zehhirah,* n. 65. The Christian chroniclers as well saw the Crusades as a time of great supernatural occurrences. See, e.g., Ekkehard of Aura, *Hierosolymita* 10, in *RHC, Occ.,* 5: 18–29, and Albert of Aix, 1.5, in *RHC Occ.,* 4:274. Also see J. Prawer's penetrating article, "The Autobiography of Obadyah the Norman Convert" (Hebrew) *Tarbiz* 45, 3–4 (1976): 286–87. Although Prawer mentions Obadyah's citation of Joel 3:4 in reference to the supernatural phenomena of the times, the medieval Jewish chroniclers, Bar Simson (as we see here) and Ephraim of Bonn (pp. 131–32, 177–78, n. 65), drew their descriptions of such phenomena from Talmudic and Midrashic sources. See, e.g., B. *Sukah* 29a, and S. Lieberman, *Tosefta ki-fshuta* (4) (New York: Jewish Theological Seminary, 1962), p. 859; Lieberman, *The Tosefta,* Sukah (New York: Jewish Theological Seminary, 1963), p. 263; and J. N. Epstein, ed., *Mekhilta D'Rabbi Sim'on b. Jochai* Exodus (Jerusalem: Mekize Nirdamim, 1955), p. 16; Midrash *Yalkut Shim'oni* Exodus 188.

231 Lamentations 3:64–66.

232 Isaiah 34:8.

233 Isaiah 45:17. In the manuscript this paragraph is followed by a narrative dealing with the accusation at Blois (May 1171), an event unrelated to the First Crusade. It was included by the copyist for no known reason.

234 This final section of the chronicle serves as an epilogue, not necessarily written by the author in question, Solomon bar Simson, but possibly added later by a copyist of the Speyer community. Although the chronological ordering of events in the epilogue is weak, nevertheless the report is basically divided among three periods, namely, the origins of the community of Speyer, its experiences during the First Crusade, and its ultimate reestablishment afterwards.

235 In the text, "their street" indicates the street of the non-Jews, thus explaining the subsequent fear of revenge by the towns-people.

236 Lamentations 2:20. This verse is employed as an acrostic, with the sum of letters tallying [4]845, corresponding to the year 1084. See A. Epstein, *Jüdische Alterthümer in Worms und Speier* (Breslau: S. Schottlaender, 1896), p. 19.

Interestingly enough, a gravestone uncovered in Mainz in 1899 bears an inscription possibly relating it to the Meir Cohen of the chronicle. It relates the death of a martyr of the same name with the burning of a synagogue and the destruction of Scrolls of the Law. The precise date of the inscription is unclear. See S. Levi, *Magenza* (Berlin: Menorah, 1927), p. 28.

237 Rabbi Meshullam may have been either the son of Rabbi Moshe or the father of Rabbi Kalonymos, the latter being the head of the Jewish community in Mainz during the Crusades. See Epstein, *Jüdische Alterthümer*, p. 20, n. 4.

238 The text is ambiguous and rendered in accordance with B. *Rosh ha-Shanah* 18b.

239 This may allude to Bishop Rüdiger, who granted privileges to the Jews of Speyer in 1084. See Aronius, *Regesten*, No. 168.

240 This is an additional reference to John, the bishop of Speyer, who protected the Speyer community from the Crusaders. See above, n. 6, and Aronius, *Regesten*, No. 183.

241 It is not clear who "the oppressors" mentioned in the text are. This phrase may refer either to the Crusaders themselves or to the local mobs who continued to annoy the worshipers even after the Crusades.

242 *Beth midrash* is a house of learning and prayer.

243 Elul is the twelfth month of the Jewish calendar, varying between August and September.

244 The copyist mentions the completion of the erection of the

synagogue in Speyer in the month of Elul of the year 4864, which corresponds to 1104 C.E. It seems that the construction of the synagogue was begun after the Crusaders left, when community life was restored to normal.

245   The eve of the New Year 4865 (September 1104).

THE CHRONICLE OF ELIEZER BAR NATHAN: INTRODUCTION

1   See *Bar Nathan*, n. 20.

2   Oxford: Oxford University Press, 1906.

3   They are described in full in M. Stern's introduction to A. Neubauer and M. Stern, *Hebräische Berichte über die Judenverfolgungen während der Kreuzzüge* (Berlin: Leonhard Simion, 1892), pp. vii–ix.

4   See *The Abraham Weiss Jubilee Volume* (New York: Yeshiva University Press, 1964), pp. 385–405.

THE CHRONICLE OF ELIEZER BAR NATHAN

1   Referring to the Day of Judgment. Cf. Exodus 32:34; Amos 3:14; and B. *Sanhedrin* 102a.

2   Up to this point, the chronicle coincides to a great extent with the parallel sections of Bar Simson's chronicle. See *Bar Simson*, pp. 21–22, and nn. 2–13.

3   *The Chronicle of Solomon bar Simson* records eleven martyrs at Speyer. Here the narrator mentions only ten, perhaps as a parallel allusion to the ten martyrs of the Roman rule in Palestine mentioned in the Midrash. See Midrash *'Ele 'Ezkerah* and the various Midrashim of the Ten Martyrs in J. D. Eisenstein, ed., *Oẓar ha-Midrashim* (New York, 1915), pp. 439–49.

4   A play on the Aramaic term for Speyer, *shpira*, meaning "beauteous." See *Germania Judaica* vol. 1: *From the Earliest Times to 1238*, ed. I. Elbogen, A. Freimann, and H. Tykocinski (Tübingen: J. C. B. Mohr, 1963), p. 326, and M. Jastrow, *Dictionary of Talmud Babli, Yerushalmi, Midrashic Literature, and Targumim* (New York: Pardes, 1950), 2:1616.

5   Song of Songs 1:6. According to Jewish tradition the vineyards refer to God and the guards to the children of Israel.

6   The Creator and His chosen people.

7 See 1 Kings 6:1, 37. *Ziv*, meaning "luster," is the Biblical term for the month of Iyar.

8 1 Chronicles 4:23. See also Midrash *Genesis Rabba*, chap. 8, where the text is interpreted as meaning that God consults with the souls of the righteous in deciding His actions.

9 Lamentations 2:16.

10 Deuteronomy 6:4.

11 The Bar Simson account substantiates the number of casualties mentioned here. See *Bar Simson*, p. 23.

12 Lamentations 4:5.

13 In text, *nekhdo*, generally meaning "his grandson," but also used in Tosaphist literature as meaning "nephew." See *Mainz Anonymous*, p. 104, and the Responsa of Rabbi Jacob Tam as mentioned in *Responsa of Rabbi Meir of Rothenburg* (Prague ed., 1608), No. 268.

14 Judges 5:31. Simha ha-Cohen's attempt at self-defense is one of the few mentioned by Rabbi Eliezer bar Nathan and omitted by Solomon bar Simson. See *Mainz Anonymous*, p. 104.

15 I.e., the situation has reached a critical stage. See 2 Kings 19:3.

16 See Isaiah 17:6.

17 Concerning the concept of *'Akedah*, see *Bar Simson*, n. 76, and general introduction, pp. 13-14.

18 See Isaiah 66:8. In text, *har ha-mor* "myrrh mountain," referring, in a play on words, to Mount Moriah, the scene of the Biblical binding of Isaac.

19 Isaiah 33:7. The association of this verse with Isaac is found in Midrash *Genesis Rabba* 56:7.

20 *The Chronicle of Solomon Bar Simson* reports the number killed in Mainz as one thousand and one hundred. Interestingly enough, the *Analista Saxo* (a. 1096; *Monumenta Germaniae Historia, Scriptores*, ed. G. H. Pertz, T. Mommsen et al. [Hanover: Reichsinstitut für ältere deutsche Geschichtskunde, 1826-], 6:729) reports a toll of only nine hundred, with Albert of Aix lowering the number even further to approximately seven hundred. See J. Aronius, *Regesten zur Geschichte der Juden in Fränkischen und Deutschen Reiche* (Berlin: Leonhard Simion, 1902), No. 185.

21 Indicating the presence of betrayers everywhere.

22 Psalms 50:23.

23 Jeremiah 10:20.

24 1 Chronicles 2:55. The Talmud interprets the verse in the

Chronicles as referring to scholars of reknown; see B. *Sota* 11a.
25 "Curled locks" refers to mystical knowledge. See Song of Songs 5:11 and the interpretation of Midrash *Song of Songs Rabbah* ad loc.
26 Joel 4:21.
27 Ezekiel 24:8.
28 Ezekiel 7:22.
29 Lamentations 1:11.
30 Psalms 79:5.
31 Psalms 74:10.
32 Lamentations 1:16.
33 See *Bar Simson*, n. 152.
34 Psalms 50:23.
35 See p. 91, and below, n. 42.
36 Psalms 68:23. Also see *Bar Simson*, nn. 150, 209.
37 Concerning the name Peter, see H. J. Zimmels, "Peter the Tosaphist," *Jewish Quarterly Review* 48 (1957): 51–52, and A. Scheiber, "Peter or Pater," ibid. (1958), p. 306.
38 Av is the eleventh month of the Jewish calendar, varying between July and August.
39 Tremonia is the Latin name for Dortmund in Westphalia. The story of Shemariah is told in greater detail in *The Chronicle of Bar Simson*.
40 I.e., one which had not been used for forbidden meat.
41 Lamentations 1:16.
42 S. Salfeld (*Martyrologium des Nürnberger Memorbuches* [Berlin: Leonhard Simion, 1898], pp. 420–22) maintains that the whole passage referring to the two Ellers is an erroneous addition placed in the text by a later scribe. This copyist confused two corruptions of the place-name Eller appearing in the original manuscript with two distinct villages. Thus, as a whole, this passage must be accepted only with great reservation.
43 The slaughter in the Cologne region began on the Jewish feast of Pentecost, which falls on the sixth of Sivan, and lasted for more than a month.
44 After Amos 5:16.
45 After Song of Songs 4:8, and the Talmudic rendition in B. *Sukah* 12a.
46 A possible allusion to the lament of Jephthah's daughter. See Judges 11:37–38.
47 Rendered in accordance with B. *Sabbath* 119a.

48 The passage, "Let not your foes . . . . I have trodden the winepress," is based on Isaiah 63:1-6. See S. Spiegel, *The Last Trial* (Philadelphia: Jewish Publication Society, 1967), p. 25.

49 See *Sefer Zekhirah*, n. 69.

50 Isaiah 63:6, 3.

51 The occurrences in these communities are given in more detail by Bar Simson; see pp. 62-63.

52 In text, '*adey 'erev*, "until evening," which is similar to '*eyt 'erev*, "at evening time," an allusion to the light of redemption following the night of persecution. See Zechariah 14:7.

53 See 1 Chronicles 4:23. Cf. above, n. 8.

54 See Midrash *Tehilim* 31:5, where the garments of the righteous in Paradise are described. Similar descriptions are to be found in various other Midrashim. See, e.g., Midrash *Masekhet Gan-Eden*, in Eisenstein, *Ozar ha-Midrashim*, p. 84; Midrash *Seder Gan-Eden*, ibid., p. 85.

55 Ecclesiastes 9:7.

56 Psalms 31:20, and cf. Midrash *Tehilim* (Psalms) ad loc.

THE NARRATIVE OF THE OLD PERSECUTIONS, OR
MAINZ ANONYMOUS: INTRODUCTION

1 Darmstadt National Library, Code 25, fols. 1-22.

2 See general introduction, p. 11 and nn. 12-13.

3 E. E. Urbach, in his introduction to *Sefer 'Arugat ha-Bosem* of R. Abraham bar Azriel (Jerusalem: Mekize Nirdamim, 1963), 4:101, cites a similar libel, also unusual for the period, in the city of Münzenburg in 1185, in which the Jews were accused of having drowned a Christian woman in a well. J. Aronius, *Regesten zur Geschichte der Juden in Fränkischen und Deutschen Reiche* (Berlin: Leonhard Simion, 1902), No. 223b, dates this libel in the spring of 1188.

4 Most likely, Volkmar; see Aronius, *Regesten*, No. 179.

THE NARRATIVE OF THE OLD PERSECUTIONS OR
MAINZ ANONYMOUS

1 Medieval rabbinical tradition dated the destruction of the Temple at 68 C.E. rather than 70 C.E.

2 Obadiah 1:4. This metaphor also alludes to the second part of

the verse, which prophesies the future demise of haughty nations.

3 On the persecution of Jews in France (Rouen, in particular) prior to that of the Jews in the Rhineland, see the autobiography of Guibert of Nogent, *De Vita Sua*, 2.5, in *Recueil des historiens des Gaules et de la France*, ed. M. Bouquet et al., 24 vols. in fol. (Paris: 1738-1904), 12:240 (hereafter cited as *RHGF*), and the chronicle of Richard of Poitiers (in *RHGF*, 12:411). Although the Christian sources are rich in information regarding the Crusade in France, very little indeed has reached us from the Hebrew chronicles of the time. One wonders how it was that Rabbi Solomon Yizhaki (Rashi), perhaps the greatest of the medieval commentators, who in fact lived in northern France during the First Crusade, left behind no explicit mention of the 1096 persecutions. I. F. Baer in his noteworthy article, "Rashi ve ha-meziut ha-historiot shel z'mano" [Rashi and the historical reality of his time] in the *J. N. Epstein Jubilee Volume* (Jerusalem: Magnes Press, 1940), pp. 320-21, saw several aspects of Rashi's commentary to Isaiah 53:4, 9 as relating to the Crusade. Nonetheless such correlations are ambiguous, and do not necessarily point to the 1096 persecutions. Thus, although no definitive source is found in Rashi's commentaries relating to the Crusade in France, an interesting legend comes to us from a sixteenth-century source wherein Godfrey of Bouillon is said to have asked Rashi about the eventual outcome of the Crusade. The latter of course predicted defeat. See Gedaliah Ibn Yahya, *Shalshelet ha-Kabbalah* (Amsterdam: S. Proopes, 1697), p. 36.

4 I.e., repentance, prayer, and charity. See *Bar Simson*, p. 22, and *Bar Nathan*, p. 80.

5 It seems that the Jews of Germany did not anticipate the onslaught of the Crusade and disregarded the warning of the French communities.

6 Jeremiah 27:17.

7 After Psalms 80:9-10 and Ezekiel 17:7.

8 2 Kings 18:13. The narrator availed himself of the description of the hosts of Sennacherib mentioned in Midrash *Yalkut Shim'oni*, 1 Kings, 240.

9 This statement is, of course, bitterly ironic in tone. The Crusaders were assured of exemption from the torments of Hell, whereas the chronicler suggests precisely the opposite.

10 This is a distorted paraphrase of Urban's absolution of participants in the Crusade, given in his speech at the Council of Clermont. Regarding the diverse accounts of Urban's Speech, see *Bar Simson*, n. 44, and S. Runciman, *A History of the Crusades*, 3 vols. (London: Penguin, 1965), 1:108.

11 J. Aronius identifies Dithmar with Volkmar, who was active in Saxony and Bohemia. See *Regesten zur Geschichte der Juden in Fränkischen und Deutschen Reiche* (Berlin: Leonhard Simion, 1902), No. 179, and *Mainz Anonymous*, introduction; and cf. Runciman, *History of the Crusades*, 1:136, 140.

12 Ezekiel 9:6. The Talmud, B. *Sabbath* 55a, deduces from this verse that God begins persecution in the martyrdom of the righteous. The narrator alludes to this Talmudic homily in reference to the first eleven martyrs of Speyer.

13 H. Graetz, in his *Geschichte der Juden*, trans. (Hebrew) S. P. Rabinowitz, 10 vols. (Warsaw: M. Alapin, 1916), maintains that it was because Speyer was attacked by a small band of Crusaders that only a small number of Jews were killed. However, our narrator attributes this fact to the sympathetic attitude of Bishop John and his heeding of the command of Henry IV.

14 Rabbi Moshe bar Yekuthiel, the *Parnass*, was one of the three notables to whom Henry IV addressed the document of privileges of the Jews of Speyer on 19 February 1090. Rabbi Moshe was also a known Talmudic scholar, and, like Rabbi Kalonymos, the *Parnass*, he too obtained a royal writ of protection which was to be honored by the local bishops. See Aronius, *Regesten*, Nos. 170 and 183, and *Germania Judaica*, vol. 1: *From the Earliest Times to 1238*, ed. I. Elbogen, A. Freimann, and H. Tykocinski (Tübingen: J. C. B. Mohr, 1963), pp. 329-31.

15 Actually this authorization of forced converts to return to Judaism was granted by Henry upon his return from Italy, at Ratisbon in 1097. See J. Parkes, *The Jew in the Medieval Community* (London: Soncino, 1938), p. 79.

16 In text, Guormatia, a name of Roman origins, found as one of the early medieval names for Worms. Since the name is not found in the other chronicles, its presence here is perhaps indicative of the earlier authorship of this chronicle. See *Germania Judaica*, p. 437.

17 In accordance with 2 Kings 18:21 and Isaiah 36:6. The explanation given in the Bible is that the reedstaff pierces the hand of him who leans upon it.

18 On the accusation of the Jews' poisoning of the well, see general introduction, and *Mainz Anonymous* introduction.

19 The "manumitted servants and maids" of the text were pagan slaves converted to Judaism by their masters. By a privilege of Emperor Henry IV on 19 February 1090, the Jews of Speyer were permitted to maintain pagan slaves (Aronius, *Regesten*, No. 170). Talmudic law encourages Jewish masters to manumit their slaves, and, with the slaves' consent, convert them to Judaism. See, e.g., B. *Berakhot* 47b, B. *Gittin* 38b; and cf. S. Assaf, *Be-'Ohalei Ya'akov* (Jerusalem: Mosad Ha-Rav Kook, 1943), pp. 224 ff.

20 A mystical combination of the verses Exodus 14:19, 20, and 21, each having seventy-two letters, implies the attribution of seventy-two names to God. See the exegesis of Rabbi Abraham ibn Ezra, ad loc., and the commentaries of Rashi and the Tosaphists, B. *Sukah* 45a, "'*Ani Ve-hu*, etc."

21 Based on the Aggadic dialogue between God and His angels appearing in B. *Sabbat* 88b.

22 Deuteronomy 26:17.

23 Burial of the dead, especially martyrs, is regarded by the Jews as a communal obligation and a behest of high degree. See Bar Simson, p. 43, and nn. 110, 111; and the Talmudic sources in B. *Berakhot* 48b and B. *Ta'anit* 31b.

24 Based upon Genesis 21:16. In all probability this narrative seeks to draw parallels between its events and the Biblical birth of Isaac to Abraham and Sarah in their old age and the ensuing episode of the binding of Isaac.

25 Isaiah 64:11.

26 See *Mainz Anonymous*, introduction, p. 98.

27 In accordance with Isaiah 31:4.

28 After Proverbs 31:31.

29 Psalms 17:14.

30 Isaiah 64:3.

31 The Great Luminary in the Garden of Eden promised to the righteous is described in Midrashic literature. See, e.g., Midrash *Seder Gan Eden*, in J. D. Eisenstein, ed., *Ozar ha-Midrashim* (New York, 1915), pp. 83–85.

32 An allusion to the advent of the Messiah. See Daniel 11:35.

33 After Ecclesiastes 9:12.

34 The ambivalent attitude of Ruthard, archbishop of Mainz, reported in the *Mainz Anonymous* is corroborated by the account in *The Chronicle of Solomon bar Simson*. See also Aronius, *Regesten*, Nos. 185-87.

35 See *Bar Simson*, p. 27, and n. 48.

36 On the lukewarm attitude of the local burghers toward the Jews, see *Bar Simson*, n. 29.

37 The belief that at night the souls of the dead pray on behalf of the local communities in the synagogues is mentioned in *Sefer Hasidim* [The book of the pious], ed. J. Freimann (Frankfurt a.M.: M. A. Wahrmann, 1924), no. 711. See also S. Eidelberg, "The Solomon bar Simson Chronicle as a Source of the History of the First Crusade," *Jewish Quarterly Review* 49 (1959): 284.

38 See *Bar Simson*, n. 31.

39 In accordance with 2 Kings 13:7.

40 See *Bar Simson*, n. 57.

41 In text, *ḥaẓa'im*, or "halves," referring to marks. The term *ḥaẓa'im* in this context is a vestige of the earlier Carolingian period, when marks were equivalent to *media libra*, "half-pounds" (hence *ḥaẓa'im*, or "halves").

42 Exodus 19:15.

43 Lamentations 2:1.

44 This refers to the belief that men of outstanding righteousness and piety are capable of intervening before God on behalf of their brethren and even of overriding a Heavenly decree. See B. *Sotah* 47b–49b.

45 The anonymous donor is said to perform the highest form of charity. See the *Mishneh Torah* of Maimonides, *Hilkhot Matnot 'Aniyim* [Laws of charity] 10:8.

46 *The Chronicle of Solomon bar Simson* attributes the Jews' defeat to a skillful ruse on the part of Emicho and the burghers, and to the weakness of the Jews engendered by their fast.

47 On the explanation of this allegory, see *Bar Simson*, nn. 86, 87.

48 Exodus 24:7.

49 See *Bar Simson*, n. 70.

50 In accordance with Proverbs 10:25.

51 On such derogatory references, see *Bar Simson*, n. 10.

52 The sequence of events in the *Mainz Anonymous* is disordered. Through comparison with the more cohesive account in Bar

Simson's chronicle, it becomes clear that the mother's spreading of sleeves between the two brothers occurred after they had been killed (*Bar Simson*, p. 36, and n. 91), as a reference to the ancient sacrificial ritual.

53 Hosea 10:14.

54 See *Bar Simson*, n. 94.

55 Psalms 113:9.

56 Lamentations 1:11.

57 In text, *lehallel*, an ambiguous infinitive which implies either "to desecrate" or "to play the pipe." It is possible that this refers to the Crusaders' custom of shouting and merrymaking after a victory. See *Bar Simson*, p. 38.

58 In text, *burkriva*, a corrupt transliteration of the German *burg-graf*, or the fortress of the count.

59 The final statement of Moses bar Helbo to his sons is fashioned after that of Rabbi Yohanan ben Zakkai: "There are two paths before me, and I know not in which I shall be led" (B. *Berakhot* 28b).

60 On the rending of garments as a sign of mourning, see *Bar Simson*, n. 97.

61 In text, *'Adir 'Adirirum*. Regarding this appellative of God, see L. Zunz, *Die Synagogale Poesie des Mittelalters* (Frankfurt a.M.: Kaufmann Verlag, 1920), pp. 475, 499. Also see Midrash *Hekhalot Rabbati*, chap. 17, and Eisenstein, *Ozar ha-Midrashim*, p. 117. Cf. B. Klar, ed., *Megillat 'Ahima'as* [The chronicle of 'Ahima'as] (Jerusalem: Tarshish, 1944), p. 13.

62 The narrator hints at the mutual cooperation between the burghers and the Crusaders. See *Bar Simson*, n. 29.

63 The corresponding passages in *The Chronicle of Solomon bar Simson* are more elaborate than the account given here. See *Bar Simson*, pp. 42–43.

64 They were among the great scholars who were martyred during the Hadrianic persecutions (135–138 C.E.). See B. *Berakhot* 61b, and cf. *Mekhilta Mishpatim* 21:13. On Rabbi Akiba as a symbol of martyrdom, see *Bar Simson*, n. 170.

SEFER ZEKHIRAH, OR THE BOOK OF REMEMBRANCE,
OF RABBI EPHRAIM OF BONN: INTRODUCTION

1 See *Sefer Zekhirah*, p. 124.

2 Ibid., nn. 11, 14.
3 J. Aronius, *Regesten zur Geschichte der Juden in Fränkischen und Deutschen Reiche* (Berlin: Leonhard Simion, 1902), No. 245.
4 See *Mainz Anonymous*, introduction.
5 See *Sefer Zekhirah*, n. 63.
6 Ibid., n. 65.
7 Ibid., n. 59.
8 Ibid., n. 68.

SEFER ZEKHIRAH, OR *THE BOOK OF REMEMBRANCE*, OF RABBI EPHRAIM OF BONN

1 Four copies of the *Sefer Zekhirah* exist in manuscript form, appearing in the same manuscripts as those of Bar Nathan's account of the First Crusade, usually following the earlier chronicle. See A. Neubauer and M. Stern, *Hebräische Berichte über die Judenverfolgungen während der Kreuzzüge* (Berlin: Leonhard Simion, 1892), p. xi; H. Graetz, *Geschichte der Juden*, trans. (Hebrew) S. P. Rabinowitz 10 vols. (Warsaw: M. Alapin, 1916), 4:464-66 (see also there the notes by Zvi Hirsch Jafeh); A. M. Habermann, *Sefer Gezerot Ashkenaz Ve-Zorfat* [The persecutions of France and Germany] (Jerusalem: Tarshish, 1945; reprint edition, Ofir, 1971), pp. 115, 255; "Piyyute R. Ephraim bar-Ya'akov Me-Bona" [The liturgical poetry of Rabbi Ephraim of Bonn] in *Yediot ha-Makhon le-Ḥeker ha-Shirah* 7 (1949):217-96; and *R. Ephraim bar Ya'akov: Sefer Zekhirah* [The book of memoirs of Rabbi Ephraim bar Jacob of Bonn], ed. A. M. Habermann (Jerusalem: Mosad Bialik, 1970). See also E. E. Urbach, ed., *Sefer 'Arugat ha-Bosem* of R. Abraham bar Azriel (Jerusalem: Mekiẓe Nirdamim, 1963), 4:39-51, and S. Spiegel, *The Last Trial* (Philadelphia: Jewish Publication Society, 1967), pp. 137-52.
2 The Hebrew of the poetical exposition is in acrostic form, the opening letters of the consecutive phrases yielding the author's name: Ephraim bar Jacob.
3 On the Hebrew appellative of God, *'el 'adirirum*, see *Mainz Anonymous*, n. 61.
4 A play on the name of the Philistine city which in the Hebrew

resembles the verb *shadod*, "to pillage." Compare Isaiah 20:1. This is to say that Satan appeared in the guise of the Crusaders in order to pillage the Jews.

5 See Numbers 33:24, 25. The Hebrew noun *haradah* means "fear" or "terror." The Crusaders traveled in groups, and their appearance everywhere instilled fear in the Jews.

6 Regarding Raoul or Radulf the Cistercian, see W. Williams, *Saint Bernard of Clairvaux* (Manchester: Manchester University Press, 1935). Our narrator used the German variation of the monk's name, Radulf, because of its similarity to the Hebrew verb *radof*, "to persecute."

7 Although there is a faint similarity to the Hebrew of Numbers 32:42, the emphasis in this context is on the gerund *navoah*, meaning "barking." This term is used frequently in describing the verbal polemics of anti-Jewish clergymen. See S. Eidelberg, "Teshuvah lo noda'at me-Rabbenu Gershom Me'or ha-Golah" [An unknown responsum of R. Gershom Me'or ha-Golah], *Talpioth*, 6, nos. 1–2 (1953): 1–2.

8 This is to say that Radulf's diatribes incited the masses, who are allegorically compared to the snake and the dog, inflamed against the Jews. See B. *Sanhedrin* 76b, and compare the homily based on Jeremiah 8:17 and Numbers 21:6 found in *Yalkut Shim'oni Jeremiah* 279, where it is stated, "I will incite the nations against you, who are compared to snakes."

9 The text states that fifty years had not passed since the occurrence of the First Crusade (1096–1146).

10 A comprehensive account of Bernard's activities in the Crusades is given in J. A. Brundage's *The Crusades: A Documentary Survey* (Milwaukee: Marquette University Press, 1962), pp. 86–96. Bernard, as leader of the Cistercian order, exerted considerable influence on his disciple Radulf, also a Cistercian. On St. Bernard's denunciation of the actions of Radulf in his reply to Henry, archbishop of Mainz, see Williams, *Saint Bernard of Clairvaux*, pp. 259, 266–67.

11 Psalms 59:12. The chronicler's version of St. Bernard's address seems to be based upon *Epistolae* 363, 365, in J. P. Migne, ed., *Patrologiae Cursus Completus: Patrologia Latina*, 221 vols. (Paris, 1844–55), vol. 182, cols. 567, 570 (hereafter cited as *PL*). The theological approach toward the Jews echoes the earlier attitude of Pope Gregory the Great. See *Epistola* 1. 47 in *PL*, vol. 77, cols. 509 ff.

12 Possibly this reference to Bernard of Clairvaux, if taken literally, dates the chronicle after 1174, the year his sainthood was declared. See below, n. 55.

13 This explains the subsequent rescue of the Jews in the fortress of Wolkenburg. See pp. 123–24.

14 An allusion to the epistles of St. Bernard mentioned in n. 11, above. In late October 1146, St. Bernard did indeed leave Flanders for Germany to quell the inflammatory activities of Radulf. While there he directed his efforts toward inducing the Germans to join the Crusade. See K. M. Setton, gen. ed., *A History of the Crusades*, vol. 1: *The First Hundred Years*, ed. M. W. Baldwin (Madison: University of Wisconsin Press, 1969), chap. 15, pp. 472–79, and S. Runciman, *A History of the Crusades*, 3 vols. (London: Penguin, 1965), 2:254–55.

15 Elul is the twelfth month of the Hebrew calendar, varying between August and September.

16 Concerning the situation of the Jews of England in those days, see C. Roth, *A History of the Jews in England* (Oxford: Oxford University Press, 1964), pp. 9–10.

17 A series of fragmented verses. See, e.g., Hosea 9:7; Lamentations 4:18; Ezekiel 37:11.

18 Compare the syntax of the Hebrew to Exodus 14:10.

19 In text, 4906. However, this would date the events at Cologne in the fall of 1145, a year earlier than recorded; most likely the correct reading is 4907.

20 Archbishop Arnold of Cologne. See J. Aronius, *Regesten zur Geschichte der Juden in Fränkischen und Deutschen Reiche* (Berlin: Leonhard Simion, 1902), No. 250.

21 A location to the southeast of Cologne in the province of Sieg.

22 In these times, Lorraine was a region of varying boundaries, including the locations where the assaults took place. See *Bar Simson*, p. 62, and n. 198.

23 They feared betrayal from the non-Jews, such as had occurred during the First Crusade. Therefore they demanded that all Gentiles leave the fortress.

24 The non-Jews were of the impression that all the Jews had gathered in Wolkenburg. They therefore ceased their harassment, and other Jews gained safe refuge.

25 After Deuteronomy 28:50.

26 Daniel 12:2, and cf. Isaiah 66:24.

27 In text, *kol 'asher lo*, meaning "all that belonged to him,"

apparently referring to the Crusader. Through the context, however, the correct reading is *lahem*, or "of theirs," referring to the two Jews whose property was confiscated.

28 I.e., God. The Hebrew construction employed here, *vatasi'aym*, meaning "and [the decree of the Almighty] tempted them," is the same used above in reference to the two boys, Abraham and Samuel. It is the intention of the narrator to indicate that just as the two boys were lured to their deaths by their youthful curiosity, these Jews went to their deaths by the predestination of God.

29 See Song of Songs 1:3. The author utilizes a Midrashic play on the words *'alamot*, "maidens," and *'al-mavet*, meaning "unto death." See Mekhilta 15:2 and the further elaboration found in Midrash *Song of Songs Rabba* 1:22, which expounds this verse in reference to martyrdom. See also *Bar Simson*, n. 168.

30 The events at Mainz took place in September–October 1146; King Conrad III, however, yielded to St. Bernard's plea to take up the cross during Christmas 1146, and departed only the following May, by which time most of the persecutions had ended. Evidently, Ephraim erred in dating the departure of the king. See Otto of Freisingen, *Gesta Friderici, Monumenta Germaniae Historica, Scriptores Rerum Germanicarum*, ed. G. H. Pertz, T. Mommsen et al. (Hanover: Reichsinstitut für ältere deutsche Geschichtskunde, 1884), pp. 60–63, and *Vita S. Bernardi*, in *PL*, vol. 185, cols. 381–83. See also Aronius, *Regesten*, Nos. 233, 243.

31 A similar plangent evocation of God is found in the mournful poem of Rabbi Isaac bar Shalom, "'Ayn Kamokha ba-'Ilmim" [None so silent as Thee], in Habermann's *Gezerot*, p. 113, based on the Midrashic interpretation of Exodus 14:11 and Psalms 86:8 found in *Mekhilta* 15:11.

32 A location on the lower Main River.

33 A reference to the cursed water of the unfaithful wife. See Numbers 5:18, 22.

34 Adar is the sixth month of the Jewish calendar, varying between February and March.

35 On the events at Würzburg in late February 1147, see *Annales Herbipolenses, Monumenta Germaniae Historica, Scriptores*, ed. G. H. Pertz, T. Mommsen et al. (Hanover: Reichsinstitut für ältere deutsche Geschichtskunde, 1826-), 16:3; W. von Bernhardi, *Konrad III* (Leipzig: Duncker and Humblot, 1883),

p. 544; and Aronius, *Regesten*, No. 245. The non-Jewish sources confirm Ephraim's account.

36 As this accusation was made in the early spring, a time when rivers flood their banks, it is possible that the Gentile had drowned while crossing a river, and the townspeople availed themselves of the opportunity to slander the Jews. The Crusaders and the burghers took advantage of this situation to attack the Jews. A similar libel took place at Münzenburg, also in the month of Adar (either 1185 or 1188), in which the Jews were said to have drowned a Christian woman in a well. See *Mainz Anonymous*, introduction, p. 98.

37 Based on Genesis 40:10.

38 Literally, a marking out with the compass, as in Isaiah 44:13.

39 The circle used as a metaphor for the souls of the dead, as found here, was employed as a figurative vehicle in medieval theological literature. See F. C. Copleston, *Aquinas* (Baltimore: Penguin, 1955), pp. 70–71, and G. Scholem, *Major Trends in Jewish Mysticism* (New York: Schocken, 1961), p. 117.

40 The bishop mentioned here was most probably Bishop Siegfried of Würzburg. See Aronius, *Regesten*, No. 245.

41 The narrator employs the term *Gan Eden*, which implies both the plot purchased and its purpose as a cemetery, mystically referred to as Paradise or *Gan Eden*.

42 Proverbs 22:9.

43 The fading of the manuscript has raised problems as to the place-name *Ham*. B. Z. Dinur, in *Yisrael ba-Golah* [Israel in the Diaspora] (Jerusalem: Mosad Bialik, 1965), 2 (bk. 1): 74, suggests that the term refers to Ham in the province of Somme in northern France. Furthermore, he associates the two ensuing localities with Sully, to the southeast of Orleans, and Carentan, northwest of St. Lô in Normandy. See Graetz, *Geschichte*, 6:152. However, H. Gross, in *Gallia Judaica* (Amsterdam: Philo Press, 1969), pp. 434–36, maintains the identification of Ham with Bohemia, Sully with Halle, and Carentan with Kärnten in Austria, rejecting Graetz's locations on the basis of the lack of sources pointing to Jews in those areas at that time. See also *Germania Judaica*, vol. 1: *From the Earliest Times to 1238*, ed. I. Elbogen, A. Freimann, and H. Tykocinski (Tübingen: J. C. B. Mohr, 1973), pp. 140–42. S. W. Baron, *A Social and Religious History of the Jews* (New York:

Columbia University Press, 1957), 4:300, n. 39, has suggested
several locations in the vicinity of Orleans in central France.

44 In accordance with Song of Songs 4:3; 6:7; and B. *'Erubin*
19a.

45 The narrator implies that the martyr will ascend to the loftiest
of the sacred precincts reserved for the righteous in the Garden
of Eden. See Midrash *Leviticus Rabba*, chap. 26, in connection
with the interpretation of 1 Samuel 28:19.

46 See above, n. 43.

47 After Isaiah 51:23.

48 In accordance with Proverbs 8:21, the verse serving as the basis
for the Midrashic homilies of the rewards of the righteous. See,
e.g., Midrash *Mishle* ad loc., and cf. *Yalkut Shim'oni Mishle*
941 and *Yalkut Shim'oni Tehilim* 774.

49 See above, n. 43.

50 On Rabbi Peter, see E. E. Urbach, *Ba'ale ha-Tosafot* [The
Tosaphists] (Jerusalem: Mosad Bialik, 1955), pp. 82-83. As to
the controversy surrounding the derivation and pronunciation
of this name, see H. J. Zimmels, "Peter the Tosaphist," *Jewish
Quarterly Review* 48 (1957): 51-52, and A. Scheiber, "Peter
or Pater," ibid. (1958), p. 306.

51 Rameru, located near Troyes, France. On Rabbi Samuel
(Rashbam) and Rabbi Jacob (Rabbenu Tam), the grandsons of
Rashi, see Urbach, *Tosaphists*, pp. 42-46, 55-80.

52 Based upon a Talmudic metaphor found in B. *Baba Bathra*
91a.

53 Micah 1:8 and Isaiah 43:20.

54 This is a paraphrase of the elegy for Rabbi Simon, one of the
Ten Martyrs of the Hadrianic persecution, found in the liturgical poem "Ele 'Ezkerah" [These shall I remember]. See J. D.
Eisenstein, *Oẓar ha-Midrashim* (New York, 1915), pp. 339-
441.

55 It may seem that Rabbi Jacob Tam was still alive at the time
the chronicle was written. On this basis, it is possible to date
the origin of the chronicle prior to 1171, the year of his death.
However, any pinpointing of the exact date is rendered difficult by possibly opposing evidence derived from an earlier
passage, suggesting the date to be after 1174. See above, n. 12.

56 A reference to the stigmata of Jesus. See J. R. Marcus, *The
Jew in the Medieval World* (New York: Harper Torchbooks,
1965), pp. 304-5.

57 At different times during the medieval period a *zakuk* was not a coin but rather a denomination in weight of gold or silver. See *Bar Simson*, n. 39, and *Mainz Anonymous*, n. 41.

58 Louis VII.

59 Actually the king granted only remission from interest and deferment of principal payments on debts owed to Jews for the tenure of his participation in the Crusade; never did he totally cancel all debts to Jewish creditors. See J. A. Brundage, *Medieval Canon Law and the Crusader* (Madison: University of Wisconsin Press, 1969), pp. 179-83. Ephraim, however, echoes the reality of the situation, for the Crusaders never repaid their debts. On Pope Eugene III's attitudes toward usury and the Crusades see his bull *Quantum praedecessores nostri*, translated in part in J. A. Brundage, *The Crusades* (Milwaukee: Marquette University Press, 1962), pp. 86-88, and B. Nelson, *The Idea of Usury*, 2d ed. (Chicago: University of Chicago Press, 1969), p. 7, n. 8.

60 This refers to the king of England, Stephen, who protected the Jews of England during the Second Crusade. See Roth, *History of the Jews in England*, p. 10.

61 Av is the eleventh month of the Jewish calendar, varying between July and August. It is quite possible that the narrator chose the fifteenth of Av for the date of the return of the Jews to their communities as an allusion to the Talmudic saying in B. *Ta'anit* 26b: "There were no feasts for Israel (at the time of the Temple), such as the Fifteenth of Av, etc."

62 Jeremiah 7:32; 19:6.

63 The narrator displays awareness of the incidence of casualties among the Crusaders. This is substantiated by general historical sources. See Runciman, *History of the Crusades*, 2:268, n. 2, in connection with the defeat of Conrad's army at Dorylaeum.

64 Kislev, the third month of the Jewish calendar, varies between November and December.

65 A solar eclipse passed over southern Europe and the Middle East on 26 October 1147 (Julian). By the Julian Calendar the New Moon of Kislev could fall in October, while by the Gregorian it is limited to November and December, as in n. 64, above. October 25 of that year was the date of the defeat of the Crusaders at the hands of the Seljuks near Dorylaeum. Evidently, the conjunction of the eclipse with the Moslem victory

created a profound impression on the European community. See T. R. von Oppolzer, *Canon of Eclipses*, trans. Owen Gingerich (New York: Dover, 1962), pp. 224, and chart 112 at end. See, too, Runciman, *History of the Crusades*, 2:268. Eclipses served as a basis for superstitious beliefs in ancient and medieval Jewish literature. See, e.g., B. *Sukah* 29a, where the Talmud treats various eclipses as portents to the future. It is interesting to note that the red color of the eclipse mentioned in the chronicle was seen by the Talmud as portending bloody battle to the nations: "If the face of the sun is red, the Sword comes to the world." See also *Bar Simson*, n. 230. Similar associations are found in other narratives of the time. See, e.g., *The Alexiad of Anna Comnena*, trans E. R. A. Sewter (Baltimore: Penguin, 1969), pp. 221, 378.

66   A location unknown to us. Possibly a vague reference to the city of Lakhish, about sixteen miles east of Gaza.

67   The author calls the Moslems Philistines. In Biblical times, Ashkelon was one of the five Philistine cities; see Judges 14:19; 2 Samuel 1:20; Jeremiah 25:20.

68   Ephraim wished to show that the Christians' defeat at the hands of the Moslems was punishment for the transgressions of their ancestors. By hinting at this explanation through a reference to a Midrashic fable, he managed to obscure his intention from the eyes of possible Christian readers:

The fable begins with the fox sending the wolf to the Jewish quarter on Sabbath eve to assist the Jews in the preparation of the Sabbath victuals and to eat with them on the Sabbath. The wolf arrives at his destination and is beaten by the Jews. Returning to the fox, he asks him why he had been beaten by the Jews. The fox replies, "They have smitten thee over thy father's transgressions." (The wolf's father had once made a similar journey to the Jewish quarter, and had greedily eaten all the best repast.)

"Shall I be punished for my father's sins?" asks the wolf.

"Yes," answers the fox, "for it is written, 'The fathers have eaten bitter grapes, and the children's teeth are set on edge.'"

See Jeremiah 31:29; Ezekiel 18:2; and Rashi on this verse in B. *Sanhedrin* 39a. See also a related Midrashic fable which interprets the song of the fox to the animals as a hint of God's future vengeance upon the enemies of Israel in *Esther Rabba* 7:3, and cf. Midrash *Abba Gurion*, chap. 3. Note also the related secular fable of the fox and the wolf in Caxton's *The*

History of Reynard the Fox, ed. D. B. Sands (Cambridge, Mass.: Harvard University Press, 1960), pp. 160–66.

69 In text, *purpurin*, a reference to the purple raiment of God; see *Bar Nathan*, p. 92, in which the related *porphyria* is employed in a similar manner. Cf. Midrash *Tehilim*, ed. S. Buber (Vilna: M. Romm, 1891), 9:13, in which the expression *porporia* is used. The context there, however, implies a derivation from the Greek *papyros*, meaning "tablet of paper," rather than the similar *porphyra*, or "purple." See *Alexiad of Anna Comnena*, pp. 17, 210, in which *porphyra* is used to denote royalty. See also Spiegel, *The Last Trial*, p. 26, n. 24.

70 A reference to B. *Sanhedrin* 49a, which deals with the sanction that the body of a hanged blasphemer must not be left upon the gallows, but rather should be buried before nightfall. Cf. Deuteronomy 21:23.

71 Song of Songs 1:15.

72 Psalms 44:23. The text includes a reference to Midrash *Sifre* (Deuteronomy, *Va'ethanan* 32) in which the martyrological implications of this verse are expounded.

73 Concerning Midrash *Lekah Tov*, see Eisenstein, *Ozar ha-Midrashim*, p. 275. Midrash *Shohar Tov* is synonymous with Midrash *Tehilim*, the chronicler referring to 31:6.

74 Psalms 31:20. See the interpretation appearing in Midrash *Gan-Eden*, in Eisenstein, *Ozar ha-Midrashim*, pp. 84, 89.

75 In accordance with Song of Songs 5:10.

76 Psalms 30:13.

77 After Isaiah 60:17.

78 This is a Talmudic reply to all questioners of the intentions of God. See B. *Sanhedrin* 111a.

Index

CPSIA information can be obtained at www.ICGtesting.com
Printed in the USA
BVOW011036110113

310078BV00001B/18/A